A FRACTURED DAMN

With passion, her lips confessed
  That I was what she always wanted and waited for,
    With those same lips, she seemed to touch my core
      From the outside in,
        Singing melodies into my bloodstream
          Like a serenade of love
            From her to him,
              She kissed me her way,
                  Savoring the pressing in twine and time
                Soft when I was used to hard gorges
                And fight was in my tongue,
She told me that it was a reflection of my love's young
  And immature stability,
    And I thought
      Immature stability?
        She told me it's full in me
          Like the nurturing of a baby
            In the bosom of the mother's reach,
              A passion that holds on to a "first"
                memory
                  So that your kiss is immersed in it,
                    And I gazed inside of her eyelid's
                      blink
And saw not my reflection
  But my self being nurtured and cherished
    In hands small yet covering my whole being,
      Kisses to my forehead and caresses to my
        Leading arm,
          Bathings in her bosom naked and warm,
            Hardened holds crumbling my fortress
              And I was open and stretched like a
              blossomed cloud,
                That was her breath—
My float was 98.6 degrees, but I felt cool and relieved
  That someone else was holding me
    Instead of me,
      And my hands felt free as they retired from their
        guard post

                    Before my mind and body
                    And then she blinked,
                        And I shook my head and saw my soul
                            separate from
                        The hip of its mate,
And my eyelid was a river dam—
    And she stood there smiling,
        Asking me what did I see,
            I told her I saw what was not of this world
                Of sorrow and hurt and tender-less hearts
                But of dreams that we sleep for
                    Knowing that it exists only before we wake
                        up
                            In sadness
                                And wash our faces with depression
Wishing we could stay in sleep and live those dreams
    Forever
        But knowing it always leaves—
            And I left her eye

...A fractured damn.

Praise for *A Poet-Whore, Pimped by Pain*:

A poetic glimpse of a cultured divided America. A staggering reality of projected hopelessness attempting to hold on to hopefulness. Casting forth images of a fallen down society and yet the rhythm is nothing new...a sense of belonging.
 —Nancy Bailey

The poems I've read were very deep. This was very interesting to see so many aspects of words in your poetry. Each poem reflected many emotions that readers can and will relate to.
 —Carolyn White
  The Associated: Jewish Community Federation of Baltimore

Thought provoking, provocative and sensitive poetry. Ka-son gets in touch with "self" through his poetry. W. E. B. Du Bois would be proud of this young Black man.
 —India Artis
  Business/ Advertising Manager,
  The Crisis magazine

Ka-Son Reeves has a lot on his young adult mind. He offers poignant, in-yo-face, thought-provoking, challenging, make you get up and do something, change your ways type poetry and prose. His work screams of the images and experiences of urban life—good and bad. At times melancholy, provocative and even erotic, Reeves always moves toward the greater good/beauty, self-realization and inspiration that we all possess. His is a growing voice that further expands the rich legacy of this literary form.

—Richard J. McIntire
Award-winning journalist, photographer, radio personality and public relations professional

A POET-WHORE, PIMPED BY PAIN

A Collection of Poetry
by Ka-Son Reeves

Whimsical Publications, LLC

Florida

A Poet-Whore, Pimped by Pain is a work of fiction. Names, characters, and incidents are the products of the author's imagination and are either fictitious or are used fictitiously. Any resemblance to actual events or persons, living or dead, is entirely coincidental.

If you purchased this book without a cover, you should be aware that this book may have been stolen property and reported as "unsold and destroyed" to the publisher. In such case, neither the publisher nor the author has received payment for this "stripped book."

Copyright © 2008 by Ka-Son Reeves

Cover art and interior art by Ka-Son Reeves

All rights reserved

No part of this book may be reproduced in any form or by any electronic or mechanical means, including information storage and retrieval systems, without prior written permission from the copyright holder and the publisher of this book, except by a reviewer who may quote brief passages in a review.

Published in the United States by
Whimsical Publications, LLC
Florida

http://www.whimsicalpublications.com

ISBN-13: 978-0-9787738-4-7

Printed in the United States of America

THIS BOOK IS DEDICATED TO THE ONES WHO HELPED ALONG THE WAY.

To my mother, Denise Reeves. Because of you, I am proud to be a Mama's boy.

To Cenia, for giving me my first writing journal and challenging me to express. You were right, two plus two *can* equal five.

Special thanks to my parents for their amazing skills in raising me the best way they knew how, which turned out to be the right way. Thanks to all of my brothers and sisters for being my circle of constant support. Thanks to Whimsical Publications for giving my work a shot. And, to my closest friends, thanks for listening, encouraging, inspiring and motivating.

A POET-WHORE, PIMPED BY PAIN

A Collection of Poetry
by Ka-Son Reeves

TABLE OF CONTENTS

1. *CHAPTER I.*

   1. —And She Said Yes.
   2. From A Meadow Frolic
   3. Episode I
   6. Why Should You Hand Me Your Heart?
   9. A Thorn In My Heart
   10. Mending A Bee
   11. Forest Fire
   12. Therapy
   13. Trapeze Artist
   15. Please Don't Play With My Yo-Yo
   17. If Only I Could, Really

20. *CHAPTER II.*

   20. Heart's Age
   22. Living In A Future Memory
   25. Who Are You Man?
   28. My Vision Is My Misery
   32. See Me
   34. When I Saw Her With Another
   35. Butterfly Kisses Away
   36. Hope
   38. A Couple In The Distance
   39. And I Say I Don't Love Her
   40. I'm Almost There

42. *CHAPTER III.*

   42. The Cycle of Languor Over Virtues Extinct

44.		She Was Cold
45.		Love Triangle
47.		Psycho Love
49.		Because I'm Still Dwelling? (An Introspective Of Love's Death)
51.		Dios Mio
53.		Therapy Session #3 — Free Association
56.		Trapped In Time

62.		CHAPTER IV.

62.		My "Mamacry"
64.		Rhyme Of Who Nursed Me
65.		I'm After Me
68.		A Man's Baby
69.		Tissues In My Backyard
70.		A Fractured Damn
72.		"Thanks For Sharing"
74.		Therapy Session #4 — Another Introspective

78.		CHAPTER V.

78.		While Along The Path Of Institutionalization
80.		Phony Homie
82.		Craziness On The Uptown 6
83.		Definition #4 — (A frustratingly or impenetrably complex system)
86.		Just 1nce On The 2
89.		Nigger Rich (angry credit nigga)
91.		Of Weed And White Powder
92.		Self-Inflicted Slave
93.		Civil Wars
95.		Sick
99.		Losing It
100.		Phony Homie (Revisited)
102.		My Mind Is Flustered

105.		CHAPTER VI.

105.		As The Rains From His Sky Poured

107.	The Best Thing I Never Had
109.	Fertile Soils
111.	Mauve Sky
113.	Lean On
116.	A Woman's Best Friend
119.	No I'm Not
121.	Dome Pluckin'

123. **CHAPTER VII.**

123.	Sunrise Capturing
125.	Kissing The Sun
126.	At A Glance
127.	Episode II
129.	Cave Woman
130.	Strummin' My Guitar
131.	Response To A Painting

134. **CHAPTER VIII.**

134.	It Must Mean I'm Falling... Again
135.	From A Meadow Frolic - Part II
136.	Caressing A Rose
137.	How Would I Have Danced?
138.	"His Plea Of Difference"
140.	I Am

148. **CHAPTER IX.**

148.	'Cause Even Now, I'm Amazed
150.	A Primitive And Ingenious Trap
152.	Friday
153.	The Hot Seat
154.	A Tropical Storm In Heat
155.	Heartbound
156.	More Than Just A Compliment
157.	My Verbal Masterpiece
159.	Love Is Forever Eternal

Ka-Son Reeves

CHAPTER 1

—AND SHE SAID YES.

Knowledge of her admiration
Intrigued his always soaring attraction to her
She defined beauty
Observing her naturalness
Caused him blissfulness
      Like ascension to clouds
Floating heaven bound from a natural high
Addicted to her aura each time he saw her
He must talk to her, she couldn't pass him by
Jitters commanded his speech as he stuttered
Only to cease when she eased
A warm "hi" arousing his mind
Lay him melted on the steps
Of their new naivety
His heart narrated tunes to her already soaring
Beats for him—
      Then he asked for her hand.

FROM A MEADOW FROLIC

A call sung from a whisper like mist's blow
In lobe tingling soft sensitive fleshes
Longing meshes like inter-opposite sensual twines
Finding connections within each other's confines
A mind lays space for eyes to wander
On fantasy grounds laced with desires to ponder
Down on knees with nose in flowered pavement
A stiffened crawl sniffing out the sacred
Infatuation
Blended like painted waters of her colored
Imagination
Vibrant green warming air breathed
Inside of relaxing beats
Like slow bass vibrating tastes of tongue tips
On petal'd pavement
Sweeter than sniffs of exotic innocent
Bushes to lay in
Environment to play in
But her call stays alluring
Luring through inhibition
A wish placed in closed lids
And shaken into her wants
Awakened heightened senses
For a carnivorous hunt—
Prey in her own playground
Breezes moan carrying
Swayed steam teases found
In her smile
And I am happily obliged.

EPISODE 1

You think I'm gonna slip pass
Without whispering jazz
...psssssss
Girl,
I have to play the bass
My vocal taste is depth
Each syllable
A note of careful composition
Stringin' rhythms to waken
Your inner submission
My vibrance your vision
Just shhhhhhhhhh baby
Close your eyes and listen

I'm lookin' around
Sight of golden gleams
Slanted fan lashes
Warm breezes of breath
Caressin' my neck

I'm sniffin' soft scents of Jasmine
Flowing from silk locks hypnotically floating me

I'm feelin' around for honest crowns
Of respect rarely found
A gentle caress to admire its presence

I'm listenin' for the wind
Of your whisperin'
And your exhalin' breath
Reaching my inner skin

I'm tastin' your smile
Pink passion lips piles
Of glee, miles of care-free
Facial imagery

Senses scream
As she intrigues sensually
Eyes tight
Visualize encounter with fantasy

Contouring body with scented petals
Sweet strawberry lips
A kiss of moistness
A hint of fragrance
Surrounds her presence
Caressing body's spark to start
The flow of inner streams
Then take a dive baby
I'm swimming between
The winding and grinding of your wild tenderness
Inhaling your body's
Most naturalness
The spasmic hip movement
Improves with rotation
With patience I paddle through
Every sensation
Foreplayin' my baby,
Our mind's adoration
Whewwwwwww...
I'm blowing a breeze
To ease your perspiration—

Damn it's hot
Should I stop
I think not
Your excitement enhances with each mattress rock
Twirl my chocolate locks
With your fingertips
Massage my lips miss
Tongue-tie me with a kiss

I'm gazing deep golden eye spells
I'm seeing your inner satisfaction girl
And I like it–
Focus on my rich brow
My thick lips as I curve a smile

Pupil is screaming
For the easing of me teasing
Your wild primal essence
I could sense heat intense deep beneath
Heads fall back with satisfaction
in our
Interaction of animal instinct.

WHY SHOULD YOU HAND ME YOUR HEART?

Hands trained to hold steady
Controlled energy
From fingertip forces
Ten sources of electricity

Gently stemmed
Slightly bent
Long and slim
Stretched out in

Anticipation to warm with
Plush cushion finger prints
To imprint everlasting love
On its large red curvaceous goddess

Pumping passionate feelings
In and out
Fingers flexible to extend and bend
Coinciding with expansion of tender

Love splendor
In and out
Inhaling, exhaling
Still holding, still dwelling...

Why should you hand me your heart?

Fingertips connect to palms
For caressing, for placing
Heart's cheek to lean against
Or heart's hand to hold

As we band forever bonded
I'll glide you through roads
With loads of unknown pleasures
We'll venture together

I'll follow you through
The desires you choose
We'll map out a plan
Goal, the happiness land

No rush, we'll seek out
The scenic route
To fill our emotions until we shout
With laughs and cries

Through bumpy rides
To appreciate our gains
On this journey, comfort
my palm will maintain...

        Why should you hand me your heart?

                Palms connect to two
                    Massive arms
              Armed with embraces
              All moments, all places

          Biceps but not by separation
            Forever together to flex
                A soft squeeze
             Not grizzly, but teddy

                    Or maybe
               If you say to me
        Growl and roar in rough desire
           My bear will bare all

            Expressions just call
           I'll protect my bear-ess
        Or caress fur soft and silky
         Never picky just pick me

                Any affection
             I'll step, stand
               Arms sway
             Any direction...

Why should you hand me your heart?

Since birth
The source of my being
Was seeing
A missed or skipped beating

From heart
A separate part
Clamp to my chain
Charge to my conduction

Power behind my potential
Connection completion essential
    Thought solo success
But heart screamed the need

What you can't do without
Describes necessary
Defines you to me
With knees kissing the ground

Arms lifted, head down
I bow to my queen
Palms with space in between
I'm the throne to your heart.

A THORN IN MY HEART

Eternal
Prick

Can't
free
or
break
from
it
because

The
thorn
is
attached
to

my
rose.

MENDING A BEE

I don't think I can stop
I have awakened many times to the desire
To run outside of my door for 100 miles
To tend to the wounded bee
Crawling in circles around my birth grounds
Because it can't fly
As many times as I analyzed the wings
And found no sign of injury
It just would not fly
It buzzes a shun when I reach to help
And I massage the lumps swelling my hands
And try to ignore the pain
Pressing deep into my bloody veins
Every time I try to ignore the buzz
I just keep getting stung
It just wants me to rest my hand in the dirt
So it could feel me steady under its feet
Warm and securing
Not moving, not changing
No straight lines
Just circles

FOREST FIRE

Eyes are ready for steady dripping
Dreary from un-granted wishes to reunite
The separation that devastated with scorching flame
The olive and lime grass dances of serenity
My leaftip stuck to hers stuck to mine
Meadow frolics though rooted footlimbs–
Unable to move, I stay in
The leftover ash, I lay in
Face dusted, difficult breaths
    I sift–
Remains of wreckage
I don't quit
Must find a life sign in my dead forest
No I won't leave
I can't move on
Without any answers
But the flames were too strong to even see
Her pull away
Striking a swift, violent magic
Smoldering all around me
Gray greenery
Windspurts burst misery
A desert meadow, and I'm still rooted
With my leaftip
now free
and crispy feeling
moistless except for the shiny teartrails it wipes
    I sift–
and find...

        nothing.

THERAPY

I'm tired of this pain
Strenuous stain
Blistering heart's main valve
Pumping to brain
Traumatizing verses
Tired of all the fucking curses
Creative energy directed by forces
Inner tears are my motive sources
Eye is dry, but book is wet
You won't expect to see my tears
Inside of here
But daily drops of sadness
Are dripping from ink
To my white-lined confidant
Look beneath—
No judgments, no opinions
Just an echo of my bellow
Absorption of frustration
Infinite patience, absolute mellow
Displaying perfect memory
Reading thoughts back to me
Learning from Self
Providing self-help
My book is my gift
Holding invaluable wealth.

TRAPEZE ARTIST

Walking with closed eyelids
Ears pressed by fingertips
She fumbled through time
Life gives a shove to blind minds
Denying
When they challenge
Right with rebellion

"Hate it when people always tellin'
    How to walk
        How to feel
            You'll never understand my real"

            But shit
            I know your deal
            Forced to walk the tight rope
            Of perfection
            With the hope
            Of success and excellence
            While mental purity is kept
            But you were denied the reality
            Of just how tight were your
            Ropes' boundaries

          Instruction, ill equipped
        Unstable can't teach stability
       Direction blind–the only advice
      Don't let that penny fall from thighs
      Trial and error now is your mentor
    Fucking up constantly just to get better
   Wonder if you'll ever learn to see
  Just how tight are your
Ropes' boundaries

A Poet-Whore, Pimped by Pain

Refusing balance beams to help your way
  Ah, damn, fell again,
    Another scar on your brain
      Why do you question a helper's motives?
       Fear that advantage
        Will ravage your focus?
         But your focus blurred now lives blind
        Without a walking stick to guide your mind
     Look behind you
    See what hurts you
   The line you walk
When traced, makes a circle
  Will you ever open, and see
    The tightness of your
      Ropes' boundaries.

PLEASE DON'T PLAY WITH MY YO-YO

Through verbal expression
The true source of his
Consistent trek
Down a path of disappointment
Became apparent—
Continuously wondered why does he
Tie self up with one end of a string
And hand the other end to another to fling
Up and down with the flick of a wrist
Throwing and pulling back
Whenever the wish—

> "Cut the string
> Remove control from the hand
> If you don't
> Forever
> Will be the clutch of the band..."

But string remains attached to chest
His will has failed to free
The current misery
For Yo-Yo's rationality
Is preservation of a fantasy
Or maybe suffrage will spark a reality
Of a life once lived so dreamily
Security and harmony
With the other end of the string

> "So spin me and pull me
> Close to thee
> When you throw me, just know me
> To spin back in glee
> Hopefully you'll wanna
> Tuck me tight inside of your grip
> Permanently—"

Now Yo-Yo's naïve sensibility
Blinds his logical mind
For the owner of a Yo-Yo
Plays only some of the time
For the enjoyment or the challenge
Of doing many tricks to test
Their skill– the object of game
To make Yo-Yo spin back; impress
Their audience

                    The Yo-Yo itself means nothing
                          When the fun is done
                                They're done
                                    With you
                                Replacing you
                        With a different fool

Left with weight of string, Yo-Yo sits
Attached to only disappointment
Hand feels freedom
Their conscience clean
If Yo-Yo only listened to reasoning
To breathe deep with bravery
Cut fast, attachment to the past
Before string pulls out
Shattering his fragile red glass
Heart

                    "SMASH"

                  Damn...

                                too late.

IF ONLY I COULD, REALLY

A claim was set
Allowing one to reflect...
A mirror in my sky scorching my second eye?

Detachment difficulty seems
To weaken one's ability
To sift between sincere and game
Sharp contrast, not, but blended gray
I can't believe that I can't see
More rumors of this fish swimming
To other ponds within her mind
I thought her past she left behind
Now normally I would not let
A negative, my mind affect
With rumors, I'll approach the source
Truth's found from mouth of horse of course
Now this horse non-chalantly nehhh'd
The truth, from rumors, not far swayed...

"I spoke those words, now ends your doubt
but of context t'was taken out..."

"But context cannot justify
with my own ear your speech was pry'd..."

"A piece of speech your ears have heard
explains why your emotions' stirr'd
still cute I did say of past men
and how I'd like to visit them
so that to them, I can declare
with you, these men cannot compare
My pledge, you did not hear to thee
But only what you wanted, see
An ounce, if you just had, of trust
You'd see that you consume my lust
The only swimming exercise
Would be with you between two thighs..."

"Love understand, adore you, I
But words alone can't satisfy
The thrust of pain that pricks me full
Forgiving start makes difficult
Now I was deemed a masochist
To place myself back into this
A disillusioned fool is said
To think that one can change their tread"

"How long can one apologize
Please gaze upon eyes' tired cries
Still plagues, the haunt of history
Inside my breast, my misery
Deserving not, of pain, you are
While carrying betrayal scars
The hourglass, I wish to take
Erase the past, one heavy shake
Improbable, but now will prove
In time, your scars, I will remove
The negatives, yes I will have
To rise above their hateful wrath—

Together, many wanted not
But longed to see two fall apart
Conspiring to end our glee
Their influence had taken me
The ways of error, I now see
Forgiveness baby, I now plea"

"Humility is easily
When one is crawling, to achieve
With haughtiness, you rode your horse
Stampeding loves with no remorse
Continuous, your trampling
'Give not a damn', your reasoning
Your thought, with horse, can handle well
When suddenly, on bottom, fell
Now your companions, with whom rode
The 'haughty posse', also known
Continued riding, helped no hand
Remember phrase 'Give not a damn'?

Ka-Son Reeves

The somber mood of loneliness
Is really what creeps through your breast
And now alone, you wish to touch
The gripping handle of your crutch
With goal, to stand alone, you'll lean
Then toss aside till next time's need
But mutiny, your crutch now screams
The 'hold up' purpose, from head clean'd–

For ages, could not live, thought I
Without the presence of your side
Hips joined, we twined in unison
Free fantasy, fly, fusion's fun
But after fantasy came then
The realization of its end
Forever joined, astonishment
When hip had split, abandonment
Regeneration of my sight
Sees now the good of solo flight
Till last, with open arms, one finds
Sincerity within her eyes
The unconditional'ity
Of honesty, trust, loyalty
For now though, love, I must defend
My heart belongs to no woman—

But don't despair, my dear, just hear
With someone, happiness you'll share
While karma seems to find us all
The lessons lifts us when we fall
From yours, advice to you, please learn
Touch not the stove, indeed it burns
Enlightened path, my goal to be
Step over past, it's history."

"I'm leaving thee."

CHAPTER II

HEART'S AGE

How do you walk with your head high
When your smile cries off the shit that your eyes grip
Females
Fucking with your mental, have you thinking
Special is your adjective
Like one head peeking out of one million closed eyelids

My bid was seven years with a lie
How do you show your face without disgrace?
In a place that you call love, solid bonds become black lace
Though transparent
Still a veil of deceit
Skill can trick a heart that a grapefruit is soft and sweet
People never understood
At least denial made that sound good
Holding in bruises
My excuses would've still stood
If I didn't keep trippin'
Klutz I didn't realize that my heart keeps bumping into doors open for the fall into
Steps and footprints
That I made before
Gotta store memories on the mind like a post-it or find
Boot prints kickin' back my behind

Ka-Son Reeves

My eyes lost sight of signs
Now twenty-eight years old with a bitter old young mind
Grumpy young man
With wrinkled young hands
Lines forming wisdom or misunderstanding above my
eye span
And now I walk slower
And bend forward when I stand.

LIVING IN A FUTURE MEMORY

I'm currently living in a future memory
My eyes are cameras
Recording constantly
The drama of life the world steadily plays
I'm losing sleep
My eyes steadily strained
Continuous astonishment
Up I try to keep
To capture every moment
I struggle not to blink
In order to believe
A visual mind really has to see...

But what about feel?
My world horrors
How do I deal?
I'm recording pain
Blood dripping rain
From leaded holes
That stole people
From people
By people
Protecting people
Or hating people
Or hating equal
Or jealous evil
The envious people
Retaliating evil
Or self-inflicted evil–

I'm rolling–

Recording my first love
Fleeing with treachery
A new love's signaling me
But I can't see her plea
Nor the passion she's offering me
Because I keep

Ka-Son Reeves

Seeking footage
Of first love and me, sans treachery
I'm rolling obsessively–
I'm rolling—
Working pressures
Wishing I was stress-free
Released from my 9-5 shacklery
This isn't free–

See my freedom delved in film rewound to youth
I often found this purest style of living
Truth—
No worries, responsibilities
Long hours flash by in "Hide and Seek"
And "Tag", "Help-Tag", "Freeze-Tag"
"Manhunt", I'm bragging
Flipping, "front sommies" over pissy mattresses but
I'm living...

And rolling...

I'm sipping watered blue quarter juices
With onion and garlic chips
And eating greasy fried rice that cost 50 cents
Though blue tongued, garlic breathed
My feel is real healthy
'Cause I'm running on happy
simplistic energy

I'm currently living in a future memory—

Now
Struggling to catch my breath
Living a fast life
Time is blurring my sense
But eyes force a focus
Trying to make sense
Of my twenty-eight year sight's
Current events–

So much talent
No ambition

Wasting life with an "acceptance" vision
A lazy son
Of work, want none
So many are praying I be the One
To use my brain to get us "ghetto-free"
But head aches, "Who's taking care of me?"
Mad mental pounding, continuous stress
From lacking an aggressive sense
Don't get me wrong
I do want my worth
If only I could get it
Without slaving first
Men wrote books on our right to be lazy
Working forty hours plus, think
That shit's crazy
No wonder we're complaining that there's
Never time
We're spending most of it
Trying not to fall behind
No ciestas or compensated overtime
An "acceptable" escape I MUST find
But until then–

My mind will keep recording
what my eyes call life...
Living in a future memory
And maybe...
It will be all right.

WHO ARE YOU MAN?

I mean damn
To try to understand
Your mental tick
Like removing cemented bricks
From wall, your shield
And when I feel
I've loosened one to peek inside
I see another brick replacing it
Open please, why must you hide?

> Nocturnal one
> Winged son
> Silent run
> Mysterious
> Flash beep, you answer call
> A dark knight
> Saving all from ails
> Exhale
> I bliss nirvana kiss
> By dawn you're done
> Blend away by morning sun
> Who are you man?

>> In you see everything
>> And nothing
>> Exclamation, and a question
>> Can tell you all,
>> Though when I ask about you
>> Silence the expression—
>> Take off your mask
>> Who are you man?

Charming creature of night
Safety, security in your sight
Carefully, a touch I take
When you respond, you stimulate
I wanna reach, though feel the fright
One inch too close, away your flight
Nocturnal wild one
Won't be tamed
By passion, companionship—
Is freedom your strength?

Or are you a fragile creature at night
Will your wings break if held too tight?
I want to fly with you
Lay back and glide with you
Be inside of you
See essence of shine in you
     Man,
               Who...
                           Are...
                                        You?

Your presence, my addiction
Do I delight in my affliction?
I know we agreed on heart restriction
But Love and Logic's competition
For control of my emotion
Snapped the hold on that devotion–
Listen LISTEN!

You're safe with me
Secure company

        REVEAL TO ME YOUR IDENTITY!!!

    Wait
                             I'm sorry
    Please
                             Don't go again
    Yes,
                             Yes I know...

You "must."

Of this furtive relationship
  I'll have to adjust
    By window of solitude
      I will wait
        while my eye inverts a white moon and black sky
          With sights afar
            Plotting my stars
              Till my heart can sing with affirmation...

Man, I Know Who You Are.

MY VISION IS MY MISERY

Her eyelids blinked a message
Louder than yells and hand-wavings
A billboard of secrecies only I was meant to see
The desire for me to come to her need
Was read by me, or supposed I think
When staring, her gestures in lid and lash form
Struck me
                But then questions of protection kept asking
                    What are those gestures really for?
                        Forbidden was the field I saw
                      Forced around her presence,
            but then again I do wear shades
              to alter the strength of reality's gaze
                          So is my sight true?
                          Can you see it too?

She extracted my heart's alluring lust
With her golden-tanned innocence
Magnificence
My poetry discovered in her beauty
Hovering over me like exotic flies
Of color bright like fairy dust
My eyes, they squint as hands they thrust
Far outside into the sky
Because she is that high,

                  I thought I was reaching for the sun
                      With my skin feeling warm
                        And my daze feeling calm
                          You know like, summer ones
                  Spent long inhaling blossomed greens
              In leaves and things like hammock'd dreams
                    Her finger reels my loins of lean
                      she's fishing for my hook on her
                        Because she is hooked too
                          Can't you see it true?

Ka-Son Reeves

I thought she was, my understanding
By me buzzed like three-time handings
Of the beach that tastes have sex on
Or its rocks with splashes so strong–
Twinkled winks and glistened hints
Of pinkish petals for the sniff
Then frolics in her inner mists
Like Jack, on Jill did
On many a night's mid,

>But each time tick I forward slick a move
>She proves my mind's been tricked again
>Like manipulated innocence
>But I am not naïve
>I mean I know my shades be on
>Distorting things at times
>But I KNOW when signs are high
>So why throw back what YOU reeled inside
>Of sight, not true?
>You mean you don't see it too?

A fisherman who reels to skill
Determine if it's present still
Is considered a merciful gamesman?
Because he throws back his catch
Like the ability was the game plan?
You see she moves her desires like the ocean waves
Of hints and clues so natural
To step inside and ride it through
The shimmer of horizon'd moons–
But when I stick a weary toe
Into the warm and wavy water flow
Back the wetness inside goes
The depth like a tide
Gone low so I can't ride—

>Is it because she wants me to just let go
>And jump a splash with passion so
>The actions of a roaring sea
>Can envelope me?
>In other words, ride

                          Whole-heartedly...
              Or are her movements just to tease
                    My ease to be hypnotically
               Seduced by bait in misty breezes
                     For a quick esteem boost?
                 Fishing line is now a noose—

Her finger linked to another life
So inside my eyes I fantasize
That she wishes it was I, just I
Because this ain't what she had in mind
Cries like eyes were diving into the storm of depression
Black and bluish forms of expression
Raccoonish her countenance
Calling for sunshiny smiles in me
That brews her jealousy
Like one in the hot sun shivering
Her eyes said to me
Before I saw them say
Set me free—

                        Perfection seen with me
              Inside the field I now look out of still
                     Like a gazer admiring her art
               Regrettin' that I didn't John Hancock
                 The piece she now flaunts around
                      For the entire town to see...
                         My vision is my happiness
                           My vision is my misery

My walk that's seen as floated leans of confidence
Is not by means of any strut
Just weary stomps and strides
Just searching for where hides
That smile from inside
Where my body's beat resides
It hides
It's been some years
But tears appear still there
At times when I can't share
Like bubbles flowing through the air
My troubles because of haunting fears

Of vulnerability
It is a new insecurity—

                        Mama does a man
               Forfeit his pants if he can't stand
          To stay away from love that's sick and set
                  With surfaces of disrespect,
            When does trust come into play again'
              When sins became the way to live
                    Deadly ocean waves
           Are why one fears to swim these days
               The heart can't drown again,
You see I still consider this "letting go" thing
                      The beginning of
                           The end.

SEE ME

        Grabbing and pulling
       Like she's kneading dough
       To mend a heart shape
          Saying,

"Kase erase the fears
From a bad experience
  Your tears on soaking fabric,
Just smear my heart
And see what happens there–
Wanna polish you a smooth present that glistens
  Like the moon shimmerin' surfaces of black oceans
Motions of serenity
  Deep breathes of positive energy..."

Not many ones were deep message senders
Forever singled out by
Eye, a standout like a sore thumb
She's tired of the walls up
"it's all good..." but really not
Saw me blinded by fairy tales and fantasies
Wishin' soon past will come back to me
Whisper three-word pleasantries
Ever after, live happily
But filled with love proven false
Fallen from my clouded horse
Stampede of reality trampled through
Mind with no remorse...
She said,

"it's beyond this span of time
Leave behind, the way that you were
Is now dead
That dove has flown a cherished home nested deeply in your head
Let it rest
Keep your focus on the new egg hatching a Dovelet–
A dovelet
—And that's me
Ready to soar infinity
But for real
Wings of love spread seriously
Selfless
Effortless
A warm feather
Cuddle heart inside my comfort hand."

As she cuddled me.

WHEN I SAW HER WITH ANOTHER

Increased thumping
Chest contraction
Filled with pumping,
Red fluid energy in a rush through tunnel vein
To main ventricle battery
Charging power within me
Bursts of plasma shoot out
Lightening bolts throughout
My body
Hands clenched uncontrollably
Trembling from head to feet,
Heavy breaths of oxygen
Lungs are forcing me to breathe,
Anger
      Fear
           Pain
                Hurt
Emotions
Combined is causing this metamorphosis
Into a beast enraged
Maybe even a bit deranged
Wanna smash all that caused my craze
The Id is reared
To make madness in my head
But instead–
Lids close in desperate concentration
Head tilted downward in and exhale
Expand chest
Meditate on new joys
My new joys
Where are they?
Id don't take control!

                    This time.

BUTTERFLY KISSES AWAY

Fingertips touched lips
Directing a soft blow of passion
Closed lashes dreamed the butterfly kiss forward
Guiding its rosy pink wings
As it floated to the one it adored—
Often I received the tiny flying messenger potent with passion
But now, who's the receiver?
Me, I keep believing
Bobbing and weaving other butterflies
With eyes set on the one in particular
To touch the lip as a tickler
Outside now, looking into the reverie
I was once in
Begging and pleading to be let back in
Chasing
With hands curved to catch eyes cornered
On fantasy
Trying to find reality
Life's variety of butterflies blurring by me
Enclosed in an hourglass of kisses I can no longer catch
Rosy pink wings swirling in bliss
Around a new receiver of my wishes.

HOPE

       A life full of fears
       In pairs, I've shedded tears
       Clouded head, confused
       This much to me seems clear—
Dissatisfied with much
Desires, hands can't touch
Them all at once, I'm stuck
Trying to grab them all
       They're falling from the bunch
       Please help me draw a plan
       A stable road to stand
       An independent man
With mind a hundred grand
Potential, infinite
Ambition, little bit
Hate persistence, but they say
Hunger brings benefits

       Too old, am I to ask
       For guidance, for protection
       Where is MY hip companion
       To help me with life's lessons
Responsible, I be-
Succeed when taking care
Of another human's needs
But falter
When the self
       Is put in front of others
       Counseled many right directions
       But questioned
       My Self sessions
       Fear of risking misdirection

No responsibilities
But living much too carefully

      They say a mind is great
      Sometimes I think it's true
      But underestimate
      Too much it's potential
Again I question Self
The fear of failure's
Why I haven't moved from here
Stares deeply rooted
      Yes
      Focusing all my breath
      Thoughts, a new reality
      All the hope that's left.

A COUPLE iN THE DiSTANCE

             When   greet
      Touch of palm   sparks energy
      Shooting with   pulsing power
         Subtle, soft   chilling vibrations
   Quick and constant   within body
        Through bone   and blood
        Tingling spots   of sensitivity—All
              Known   and unknown
            Explored   and undiscovered
             Instant   weakness in muscles
    Visions of ecstasy   wiz by almost missed
                But   still noticed
             Cause a brief eye flutter
        Heart beat a wonder

...Where's my lover?

AND I SAY I DON'T LOVE HER

So consumed with my own scars
I'm dragging along a wisher
Wishing to see the healing form within me
So that with reopened eyes
I could realize
That Right was right in front of me
The ear
My guide
Absorption of my emotion
Her eye let out my tears
My hurt, my fears displaced
Into this healer's accepting face
Now she's frowning
Representing my depth of sorrow
Understanding my need for a newborn tomorrow
For now, a smile is handed to borrow
With soon a permanent one to follow
But now, just wishing
My side companion
Helping me chase the moon
Moving through blue blackness and gray clouds
Hoping to capture it's half pink radiance
Its shine
Its mine
Amongst an atmosphere of gloom
That gleam of light pries through
The answer, she says
    "don't let it leave forever,
        chase it down, with diligence now,
            don't lose its glowing face—
                the light is yours to embrace."

I'M ALMOST THERE

Rubbing lids-
  Sudsy lather
    Scrubbing face
      A shaven place
        Awaken state
          Eye steady peeling
            Focusing on reborn feelings
          Now revealing
            Mourning time is at its ending
          Realize to stop pretending
      Gargle fast
        Then spit out past
      Refreshing mouth can breathe at last,
Energy
Is surging through my arteries
Replacing emptiness with glee
Removing pain
  My heart is pumping
    Once again
      I feel no strain
        Now when I bend
      "Eureka"!
          I found a new friend
          Or two
            Who helped me through
        My ditch
        To picture brighter
      Sunny strips

  —I'm gripping ends
So I can blend
Within the love
I'm being sent
  I'm finding strength
    In numbers
      All around me
        Family and others
          Many hands

                But one in ditch
                    That's powerful enough to swiftly
                Twist me, screw me
          Back inside
            Enticing me- desire cry
        I'm blinded by her mask
      I'm hurting
    Help me solo fight ain't working
GET ME OUT OF HERE!
I plea
Assistance free me misery
      With hustle 1 and 2 and 3
        With muscle pulling myself free-

            I'm out at last, I give a thanks
            I over glance, appreciate
            The company
              Who helped me
            From my ditch
            Remove the lather
            Rubbing lids, eyes steady peeling
          At the face reflecting back
      A shaven face
    A newer face
Of peace and grace
You're blessed
With friends
    Who showed a hand is lent
      When self is spent
        Now nod I nod
          A wink reflection winks
            Then smiles
              I think I'll look beneath
                The self
                  To find a heart rejuvenating health
                And deep inhale
              My newborn air
            And step my new path
        With no fear–

I'm almost there.

CHAPTER III

THE CYCLE OF LANGUOR OVER VIRTUES EXTINCT

Heart swiped before his eyes
He couldn't see it
Mind manipulated by lines
Could not believe it
She crept up in between his arms
And with her charms
She did a belly dance
That set no alarms
No protection
She accessed his security sequence
By the section
The walls he built around
She tore down
With her affection
The baited bush enticed a look
Hook lined and sunk
Now he's struggling shook
Upon this love hook
Set for the stripping
Peeling off his armor revealed
The sensitivity
Massaging mental keenly to reach
His heart's virginity
Secure, eyes closed, now under nose

The dirt is done
Until he opens eyes
To find he's alone
Chest throb and weary
What the fuck just happened to me?
Becomes the query
Emptiness is pumping through blood
Pains sharp and steady
Clutching chest for breath
As he screams
His eyes are teary
Time in silence
Head he lifts
Emotions gone
The dog is born
To pray on new innocence.

SHE WAS COLD

Blistery leather
    Comfort collar swaying pushing
–Calm down Cold man
Damn

Leave me alone
    I'm on the phone
        Telling love life, I'm comin' home

    Frosted fingertips–
        Frozen Tele-grip
"Do you love me?"
    "Should you doubt me?
        Who's bravin' blizzardry gusts?"

I said stop pushing me Cold
It's just us baby, what's the fuss?

All right, you win
You're felt within
    The geese are rising on my skin
      in time to chime the end of my 3rd minute

    Un-grip the tips
        Receiver click
Wipe liquids leaking from nose to lip

    –I'm outta here.

LOVE TRIANGLE

"I'm in love you," they said
Tri-angular expressions
Ear lobe-to-lobe receptions
Received in multiple directions
Emotions
Ache, pain, joy, surprise, annoyance,
My mad neck shifting
Constant left and right
To listen to their heart's thoughts
Call it a tug fight
Pulling my brain tied by vocal cords meant to
Desperately make one's love for one's self central
Left anger, right tears
Different extremes of similar fears
Powerful eyes, six rotating stares
Please see into my mind, feelings flesh out of here—

One dared to create a triangular love path
Bending a straight line
Trying to defy the laws of math
Set to prove with a philosophical mind
That if you take control
Two and two can equal five
Road is now set, trek in ignorant bliss
Oblivious to what reality will ultimately dish
Enjoying the laughter
Deep penetrating
Mind interaction
Feelings awaken
Back and forth to each attraction
Not seeing past the present satisfaction...
Triangles tend to cause drama, once was told
But ego claimed control of angles
If drama unfolds
Thus became the philosophy of the naïve
Tingled web of deception
He unknowingly weaves
In exploration of selfish desire
Greed blind as hand dipped
And burned
Inside the fire.

PSYCHO LOVE

Under the cover of dedication
Fear sleeps with a knife
                      Held close like a heart's protector
                       To keep it whole like a forced mend
Enslaved in fatalistic passion
Who needs space
                                An eager race
  No one else must be in this place called our sacred bed
Where secrets shed bruised blues
We sing together
                           But I know you love me
      Though your affection is hugging my cheeks hard
With closed hands like slamming down
Thoughts on the table
                                   My chest
                              Aching breasts
But you love me so much you must squeeze a
passionate wound
                                    Closed
                         In like my knife
A heart's protector
No no no no
                     Don't you dare go nowhere
                      My eye's not yet closed
By your expression of despair
Or should I say fist full of kisses
                     Like blowing my wishes
                               Away
Calls to leave by loved ones, please
Our understanding they can't conceive
        Not even my therapist can keep me from you
            Or the restraining order we both looked to
But that was just us playing
                Under my bed courage is gaining
                     To display the ultimate act I'm praying
Reciprocation
For the stabbing your thrust goes into my womb
                Then stepping my future a fetal doom
                But love is to do as is done to you

And you love me, but I am longing to show you
I love you, under my bed my last
                                              Secret
                                  I'll embed forever
A final bond we'll forever treasure
You'll come home cologned in vodka'd aroma
                    And force your love with a physical thunder
                            Then sleep will fall you top of me
And I will pull from under the spring
Like a glow
                                a sharp symbol of my love
                                    To pass through us slow

BECAUSE I'M STILL DWELLING?
(AN INTROSPECTIVE OF LOVE'S DEATH)

>   To wonder of times when smiles would climb
>   Upward in lines rounded like a stringed swing
>   Attached to happy things twinkling in slanted
>   Thin eyelids
>   Passion is pondering gazes
>   Still but still amazes like movements swift like blurred
>   images

Of hand holding and showing how touches spark glowing
Knowing this exists no more beyond the
Reminiscences
Plagues the one who now chooses
To live their life in dreaminess
The past nostalgic is the logic spoken with
Enthusiasm
Not fathomed by those who see the crazy glee and call it
Insanity
They even pointed fingers at me as I walked among
them

>   Proudly

Yes I am a man insanely in love
With a mirage of memories misting me
Distracting me from any possibility
Of seeing any other hers, my healing is hope less hope
Mess I've gotten self into
So deep, I patted the graveled ground
That I seeped into under the depth of my sixth footprint

So my eyes blink bland blood shot red hands
On my head
Because reality's got me gripping brillo hair strands dead
And red
And she said we were meant to be
While SHE said I was meant to be free
But then SHE said I was meant to see
Her instead of the other three
And that included me

                    I never gave my whole to any one
              After I lost my soul absorbed in one
    None had a chance or could even reach into my groan
       No matter how hard we made each other moan

I'm stressing this multiple distraction of emotions
Not knowing what I want in whom while I got
This piece here, and I'll take that piece there
And use 3 women for each of the things that I love in them
Like a buffet I pick and move or stick and move
To fill my plate with hot portions
Trying to fill my tummy with the perfect meal

But still,

                                    My taste remains cold.

Dios Mio

When I dip my mind's brush into my heart
And stroke my desires over my years' scuffed canvas

Set me free

When my time second hand strikes one then four then three
Skipping or missing everything in between

Set me free

Who says I am not courageous?
My hands, that is, that contradict my mouth
When I don my brass shackles like gold bracelets
Bonded to a heart telling me
To not, would be a loss greater than itself

Set me free

I call this love
The fear of moving on, lied
By my cry for a one and only
Justifying the grueling push of my sole
Against a concrete conveyor belt
As time passes me

She put me on this step saying
This is the way to me
To walk without appearing to wait for me
Because even though in place, still you are moving...
On...

right?

And raw faith bowed a head nod in assent
Against the better judgment, I relent
To please a deity is sacrifice
Reward in future, self's a present price

In meadow beds and yellow blanket rays
And tranquil serenades her promise lays
Behind a broken trail of treachery
The past is not what lies in front of me

Although the pain pulls it's own chains
Inside a bolted cage, beating
A native prayer is danced for rains
From eyes above, but not seeing

So I stop singing couplets
And stare somberly at the wrinkled skin
Underneath the brass—growing
And the sandbag knee joints
That held my blind devotion firm
Blistering and bursting and beginning to spill
Out my belief from my prick—and I feel
Like standing and singing my own
But then here she comes again with her voice-song
Like a pied piper's flute
To string me along, once more
And I go, legs bent, knees hover like a float...

        Because

        I

        Still

        believe.

THERAPY SESSION #3 — FREE ASSOCIATION

With reluctance
The hand opened up for the flying
Of a cooped chicken trying to be free
But opposite of mind security chained her feet
To S & M her mind with fire time
Switched the place
She's Sadistin'
I'm Masochistin'
And now I'm clutching chains

She's laughing at her domineering pattern
A lonely eye is floating in a puddle of my sorrow
Until I see a couple, of my path, looking to follow
But opposite
She's locking him while he's dipping
Still slipping through her prison
For his bang-bang decision
Sibling to my chicken
Squawk in dumb, selfish unison
But who's dumbing more
Wild birdy whores
Or the keeper of around sleepers
Out storing physical memories
Used to stab the heart beneath us

But bananas in my bird's tailpipe
Tell me that her lips are not too satisfying
For a single pops, kids three he tops
His penis opts for berries
Bend Over Buddy
He slides her cherry, for a pillow buried
So she pulls my coat to seal her right
Remind her what a man is like
So shove a heartless scream
Into a soft, moist squooshy dream,

Relived without relation—Ship has sunken

To join a drowned ocean liner
Scarred from abuse and time neglect
Similar stories make our minds connect
Reflecting eyes and cries gave rise to
Resurging ties that drain the tides
Unanchoring our bodies
Transforming to sky soar
Above sea roar
The best thing and the worse thing
For second path crossed is better than the first thing,

But first's a cinder block
To second's forward ticking clock
A scandalous sort
She called it star crossed
Lovers,

So in secret we crawl into each other's... all
In time she's demanding a secret no more
I tell her our bonds, friend and blood
Won't mix happiness
That we must rethink the purpose of our co-existence
But she "ain't hearin' none of this"
She wants me to carry her luggage and mine's with her
And call this happiness
When I ain't ready for baggage claims
Arms that lifted weight now asked
To change to lifting chains and balls
She said
"If I loved her I'd gladly carry all
Forget the scandal love and friendship had
On our restricted path
A friend was lost to gain a love
But sacrifice of your blood was nothing but
Mental bluffing
Emotional hustling
Cashing in on a vulnerable body
Has become the hobby of a manless man
Who uses hands of seduction for interrupting the plan
Of a forward mover

You're a 'Self' loser
  Taker
      Misery maker
           Chain-carrying to clamp a shackle
                Bait to trap
                    Freedom breaker

But clamp won't catch the ankle of a fled dove
Free now from your dominion
So squawk your woes alone in your own selfish prison
You've become what you've hated
The male equivalent of a chicken—

                                    Sucka!"

TRAPPED IN TIME

                                        tryin' to contain
                                  mental balance
                         lips widened
                 to coincide with
          expansion of two eyelids
stunted breath-
        vocal cords try to scream
                but there's nothing left
                      why?
              foot shackled to one point
      on the line of time
eye left to watch all
        move forward, hands outstretched
              leg tries to pull
                      but I lack the strength
              to move on to the next frame
don't you see me attempting to flee

```
but I'm chained
        my time stopped
                ears tortured by
                        constant calls to come
                                forward
                        they're looking back
                as my pupil strains
        to maintain sight
of the images
        tears dripping
                look up
                        flying forward world's passing
                                she's graduating
                        he's graduating
                she's growing
        she's showing
she's showing???
```

NOOOOOOOOO!!!!!!!!!!!!!

                        not without me
                    please I'm beggin' please
                            don't keep mind stuck in time
                        frame's a torture
            hell type state
because I see her
            baking in her oven
                        another one
                            but this time she intends
                                    to finish this one
                        plans to feed her longing
                    plans to please her new chef
            for the contribution
lending the right ingredients
            what I wouldn't lend
                        question if I couldn't lend
                                does my legacy end
                                    with me
                                trapped to life's timepiece
                    paused

                                                        forever?

CHAPTER IV

MY "MAMACRY"

>>Often it isn't said or showed in depth
>>Of what one feels and knows except
> The smiles inside that climbs each time
> The holding of hands or locking of eyes
>>Ignites the warmth ascension of
>>body temp expressions love
> The skin that bubbles to ends of hairs
> It can't be explained, but it can be compared
>>To electric shocks that sparks a curious
>>Character climbing vocal barriers
> Carrying higher forms of intention
> Monopolize the forms of affection
>>That is found comfortable; selection
>>Is more of those shocks, in sections
> That is chosen when chosen but it doesn't mean
> The desire is faulty, or full of greed
>>That feeling IS loved, and in between
>>The pulses passed into the stream
>>>Reciprocation's genuine
>>>See...

A complication grabbed a chain
And cuffs to hold the heart and brain
> Inside the barren span of land
> Of bone that's cold from chills and sand
That flows, slow like calm red winds
Within then gusts when wants are sin

                    Aggressive...
                              ...no obsessively passive

Tensions; pity of self is massive
Can one feel sorry for I? For self
                Is not complete or satisfied
                It's like inside is died
It's like inside is died
It's like inside is crying red sand
                Wiping the blood with my own hands
                Held high and screaming
Look I died
Now please resurrect me
                I don't wanna try

                          Is my heart beating?
Nah, it's retreating to the cage it belongs in
                      Rib- eating at itself
Spaces in between seems to tease a release
                      Into a world of evil
The kind that you gotta play in to stay in
No matter how burning the bed that you lay in
Self, I must learn to find a way in
Without getting lost in my stream's labyrinth
                What's sad is when I want to fly
                Inside, my mind gets terrified
Like a sheltered pup placed in public madness
Called open enjoyment and world walking, fast is
        My shiver, but a slight quivering shroud
                Of coolness hangs on

                        Trust me when I say

      My cool shit is THAT strong.

RHYME OF WHO NURSED ME

Mother Goose
Laid eight golden eggs.
What's more precious?
The creation molded with glistening gold
Or the producer of those shining bright brown round
babies

      If Mother Goose can no longer create
   No
         longer
               produce

Does
That
lessen
the
value
of
Mother
Goose?

I'M AFTER ME

Everyday I find myself running
Through endless roads while coyotes close the gap
Hugging
Dust of sand flying from my feet
And hands
I'm on all fours scrambling

        Can't escape the madness as I glance back
        He's foaming, teeth showing
        Reflections
        Of the one to be stomach's ingestion
        Beat pulsing, pushing, ripping through rib cage
        As I'm huffing

Looking for some cushion of safety
Eyes flying in front of face
Too scared to stay in socket's place
Jaw stretched as tongue makes way
For lung's scream for air
Thundering growls vibrates fear into ears

        Through bloodstream like cracking glass
        Expanding through body
        Held together by arms
        Hoping to stop it from shattering
        A fetal crouch prays for safety
        Within a boulder's blanketing shadow

But the deafening howls
Spewed a stench of raw breath
Thick and misty enough to lift me and my back hairs
So I dart swiftly to meet my skin
No longer crawling but sprinting
Nowhere

        For suddenly cornered by
        Walls slammed, two pairs squared
        Windowed around me
        Blocking him out like a transparent shield
        I'm closed in a field-forced

To keep out the scratching,

Scowling, howling,
Savage shut out,
I'm shut in, looking out
As he's looking in
My glass wall
Thick and distorting my vision

                        So I rub lids for focus
                       Like a tin lamps magic wish
                  Wishing for his disappearance
                     Sudden entrance to ear
                            A swift silence–
                  One at a time, I peel open eye

And lean in
To closer see into
Wall,
Searching for him
I see nothing
Head bows down, lungs exhaling relief

                            Up looked again
                            Heart screams
                          He's in front of me!
            Through glass giving a blurred growl
              But somewhat controlled now
                  I calm as I fix our gaze

Glaring
Trying to see with clarity it seems
As I step closer he closes in until we are separated
By only the distortion of the glass wall
A trembled hand ascends and touches and wipes the glass
As a distorted paw descends from it's own wiping

                                  Glaring
                   Frightened eye to red eye
                          Fear to aggression
          We pull in closer, we wipe once more

A slow transition sharpens my vision
Mouth falls then eyes widen like an awakened nightmare

An overflowing tear escapes a damned cry.

A MAN'S BABY

        I like to walk with assurance
        Outside of my insecurity
To make that vulnerable man with the sensitive beat
          Cradle himself deep within his rib crib
          Curled on his stomach
Pulsing himself to sids' sleep

          So I can always be that other me.

TISSUES IN MY BACKYARD

I walk paths laid out by my own history
Of actions both plus and minus the nurturing of emotions
Calling out to me close and at a distance
Like distorted images in movement
Whispers difficult to make sense of
What's with these tingled webs
That's said to have been woven by my indiscretions
I called my former love an obsession
Now I'm left by her and obsessing over her and her
These are others
Trapped in lives still attached to another
And they say they want to be my lovers
If only I can have the faith of a spiritual brother
And believe in our hopes for a future—
As much as my wall was up,
I still chiseled some, believing these women
Were just a little bit different
Than my past experiences
But drama seems to vibe around my outsides
To tamper with the instability of my insides
So I can never really be satisfied—
I'm tired of looking outside of my bubble
And only reaching to touch right outside
And not traveling for my love
But I guess deep down
I do have fear
That my travels will lead me nowhere
Different than where I am over here
Can all the issues I see be centrally located in one wet tissue-infested area?

My backyard man, damn.

A FRACTURED DAMN

With passion, her lips confessed
   That I was what she always wanted and waited for,
     With those same lips, she seemed to touch my core
    From the outside in,
     Singing melodies into my bloodstream
    Like a serenade of love
    From her to him,
     She kissed me her way,
        Savoring the pressing in twine and time
        Soft when I was used to hard gorges
      And fight was in my tongue,
She told me that it was a reflection of my love's young
   And immature stability,
    And I thought
      Immature stability?
        She told me it's full in me
       Like the nurturing of a baby
       In the bosom of the mother's reach,
       A passion that holds on to a "first"
        memory
         So that your kiss is immersed in it,
          And I gazed inside of her eyelid's
           blink
And saw not my reflection
   But my self being nurtured and cherished
    In hands small yet covering my whole being,
     Kisses to my forehead and caresses to my
      Leading arm,
       Bathings in her bosom naked and warm,
       Hardened holds crumbling my fortress
        And I was open and stretched like a
        blossomed cloud,
         That was her breath—
My float was 98.6 degrees, but I felt cool and relieved
   That someone else was holding me
    Instead of me,
      And my hands felt free as they retired from their
      guard post

Before my mind and body
And then she blinked,
And I shook my head and saw my soul
separate from
The hip of its mate,
And my eyelid was a river dam—
And she stood there smiling,
Asking me what did I see,
I told her I saw what was not of this world
Of sorrow and hurt and tender-less hearts
But of dreams that we sleep for
Knowing that it exists only before we wake
up
In sadness
And wash our faces with depression
Wishing we could stay in sleep and live those dreams
Forever
But knowing it always leaves—
And I left her eye

...A fractured damn.

"THANKS FOR SHARING"

> His Turn To Share at a DDA Meeting
> (Dirt-Diggers Anonymous)

Ignoring the binds
investigation finds in the digger
of information concocted to feed a suspicion
Begging me to open the closet
Seeing if I'd find a bone or something
like a bird dark as a Crow
or dirty as a Raven
to shock me into attention
Hints seem to mention
that dirty birds favor and flock
the flattered partner of a secured Spock
If a closet is opened should it mean you must peek?
Should information not offered be a "treasure" to seek?
Should one always comment on what's in one's face?
Here's a comment, should it even be there in the first place?

Créame cuando digo, yo
puede ver, pero
Seeing and seeking is different
Curiosity kills and Satisfaction thrills
but sometimes "treasure"-hunting gets you lost and you feel
like where the hell am I?
And who have I become?
The magnifying glass on my private eye is now stuck
and I can't blink like the normal person I once was
and every other question is

        where were you on the night of...?
          So to really see, I have to wash
the private eyes of me
in acetone baths so my magnifying glass
can be removed from me, and my job as a cynic Dick
can be placed in a forced retirement
So I can try to live with a peaceful face
without my obsessing
over investigating
Hoping to find something
I didn't want to see in the first place.

THERAPY SESSION #4 — AN INTROSPECTIVE
(A long, tedious uninterrupted speech with NO conversation)

My insides are telling me
Like a whisper that haunts, no, rather
Taunts my mind to exercise itself creatively
To cling to the cliché of something about running waters and stale grows
So I'm forcing myself to flow flow flow like a faucet
Being run to remove the brown rust to just stay away from stale,

                                        Crisp and rich
            Not pale and thin like my surface verses
Or like sentences in prose, or a conversation that arose from
Nothing
So again I stress that I am writing something out of
Nothing short of spurts like the sneeze held in making my heart hurt
See I thought THAT as I felt the pain of bodily function-hiding
Using that to keep my flow riding the stream that my insides say
Is a creative being at work like
The city is full of it...

                      Shit
    I used that word because it rhymed with "it"

See that's the shit I'm talking about
Basically juggling thoughts hoping something will creep out of the spin
Of my thoughts whirling within
Scratch that, I believe I used that phrase before in my book
So that was like... um
A filler to make my line quickly go with the last
For a rhythmic effect I'll do it again fast,

Like that...
Writing to me is a purging of thoughts that your mouth
Would think twice about divulging
Or splurging without proper placement
Slight disarray and your sound's incoherent
Even though it made perfect sense inside
    When your mind read it
But you spoke your thoughts to another mind you're not one
    With
        See,

And that's where I guess miscommunication comes from
The throwing of thoughts at random like raindrops
Both in buckets and spritzes
Is it pouring or drizzling?
I guess it depends on your timing

  Speaking your thoughts with no importance on rhyming

      See I did it again

You know, that "rhyming" thing just for rhyme's sake
I used "rhyme" to rhyme to make rhythm take precedence
In my conversation
No, monologue 'cause I ain't talkin' to no one else
But myself

Words and phrases could be used to set any mood
Or words and phrases are usually set to evoke every mood
Every meaning ambiguous in interpretation
Depending on what you place in relation
Like this fortune cookie I read today
Saying
"May you grow rich"
Which is a perfect example of ambiguity
Of interpretation depending on relation
'Cause one can grow "rich" with joy or "rich" with sorrow
"Rich" with intelligence, or "rich" with ignorance

One of the 14 definitions of "rich"
Is a large supply or a mass abundance
So basically "rich" can mean FULL of it
So these cookies to me are "rich" with shit
And that's all I have to say about this...

I received beauty yesterday
from one who's beautiful everyday
We kick convos through email and phone
Until we could meet up in her or my home
With bonuses in being alone
A rose was given 12 times for me to walk with
Helping me realize
The depth of her feelings
Yellow with deep orange tips
The kind I, myself liked to give
Although I lost the remembrance to make it my present
State of representing my affection
It's like for some reason I lost that connection,

              With myself—

I mean I always knew it weakened women
To equate with roses the depth of feelings
I knew to the opposite it was appealing
I don't know, man why I stopped dealing them out
Maybe I'll reveal later in my babble—

I also compared a rose to the
Blossoming of inner thighs exposed
In fact my first poem expressed the
Similarity of petals both fuzzy and fleshly
Uh, anyway...

She gave me these roses, and I
Immediately looked around for any notice
Of eyes focused on this situation
I can't remember last being in.
Embarrassment I was sitting in
I couldn't even help my "MAN"
But I let it hide and paid no mind anymore
for in store, fun with her I'd find for sure

As we dined on eye glances and half-off foot fashions
Until it was time to part
I didn't even realize the flowers have become a part
Of my carry-on
But I carried on with a kiss to my miss but not without
Beef over this thing called me taking long to find a fitted
Kick in this shoe store
So she walked away pissed
Because our time was "wasted"
Ain't this a bitch—

My 12 pussies with stems and thorns
Pricking my fingertips as I walked on
Thinking how so much they are like "them"
So beautiful yet so full of prick
Tender and sensitive they must be handled or
They'll without hesitation stab you
They smell so sweet, but sweet enough to eat?

I've heard of rose eaters...
And I've tried...
I don't know...
I guess I'm more of a rose tweeter
But anyway with my 12-woman wrapped
I let my stride take me back to work
Like the city is full of it,

    Shit

I know you're like wait wait wait, hold up,
What the hell is a rose tweeter?
Well to tweet means to let out a high pitch sound
Like the song of a small bird
And my fingers play the loudspeaker amplifying
The sound heard
In her
Through her inner lips with my finger tips— like a
                                                "tweeter"?
                              Get it a little?
                   No?
           Whatever, who cares...
    The shit rhymed with eater.

CHAPTER V

WHILE ALONG THE PATH OF INSTITUTIONALIZATION

      Wired like a board of switches
    My mind wondering which is the way to
        Psychosis resisters
Puzzling mixtures of contemplative pictures
Gray the black and white line of reality
    So at times I'm here or there
     Depending on step's steer
     Away from going nowhere
  Lack of focus helps influence's entrance through ear
     To the front seat of one's mental faculties
Now wondering why I no longer have the keys
To drive exactly how I wish
Because they're driving me crazy
  I saw him pop her three times right in front of his baby
    "Daddy please stop! Somebody save me!"
      As tears fall, slugs fall, lives fall
        Hearts fall deep
     Unconscious, frigid and response-less
   Character corpses walkin' in my grounds too often
    Sifting the central system for a nervous mental
      Stalking
So paranoid footsteps press the same pavement
Questioning why it is that I live amongst them

And if I will ever become one
Of the products of this wonder-less existence
Descending in size to caress steps of rock crevices

In hermitous silence

Alone,

denying loneliness.

PHONY HOMIE

Why be phony, homie
                      Front like bud in my presence
                                "What's up?"
                          "How you doin' yo?"
                           "This is my bro."
            Yo how you gonna utter cool vibes
             While masqueradin' ill slights
             You wanna linger 'round my style
              Professin' love to fit this glove
       Meanwhile observin' one's humble might
                  Absorbin' it's light
                     To in time act like
                  The glove you gaze at
                    With envy, despair
         'Cause glove embraces only dear
Its clique
                         Within it's grip
                         You try to fit
       With expressions of similar interests
                Real motive kept secret
                Till I peeked past eyelid
       And seen the truth that you had hid
           Reports on how to be this kid
         Many documents I found date back
             To when I gave first pound,
In fact,
                Looking back, one can now see
     This presence was just a little too friendly
                      You latched to me
                       I felt your pull
        But didn't see yet past your wool
                   Blame to myself
                        Guard down
Unseen
       Wolf creepin' in disguised as sheep
         Big hearts can blind, let down
                          Protection
                   To welcome the

Ka-Son Reeves

                              Knife-in-Back deception
In time progression of persistence
Gave birth to a so-called "Ka-Son Thesis"
Complete with quotes, footnotes,
Goal be
                         To follow this "Ka-Sonology"
A well thought out, researched literary
Because now you're my mirror
When you strut silently by me
But distorted
Lacking insight into the power
Behind the glove's grip
Solidified bond
                                  pride on true friendship
For that's the main ingredient
Sincere Naturalness, see?
Your mirrored image exposed a false reality
Of the real that you tried so hard to copy
So take off my coat

You fabricated phony
You've been discovered.

                                      No longer my homie.

CRAZINESS ON THE UPTOWN 6

Craziness on uptown 6
Other than over-crowded stress
A woman's nonchalant mess
Hanging over, holdin' on
Swaying side to side upon
Craziness on uptown 6
Witness to her garment switch
Sneaker off, over bent
Swaying side to side we went
On the uptown number 6
Crazy over-crowded stress
She never minds, displayed no shame
For next eye saw, off sock had came
What the hell, I wish I missed
This craziness on uptown 6
Because now I'm in the midst
Of bunions, corns, and callouses
My facial squinch when saw exposed
A Band-Aid wrap on pinky toe
The gnarly nails, white flakes of crust
Disgust, get off this train, I must
Head up, eyes closed, mercy I pray
For stop to not be far away
But playback mental picture shows
The image of those gnarly toes
To haunt me deep
I'm counting toes to go to sleep
I'm seeing toes each time I eat
Forever froze
My eyes can't close
This craziness on uptown 6
A sudden twitch, my nose, what's this?
A mix of sweat, funk and corn chips
Shoot through my nostrils, fleshing rip
Back, eyes are rolled, tears start to flow
Must have air! I gotta gooooooooooooo!
Excuse me miss, I'm fleeing this
Craziness on uptown 6.

DEFINITION #4 —
(A FRUSTRATINGLY OR IMPENETRABLY COMPLEX SYSTEM)

    Many times I ask
             What the hell am I doing here?
    My goal to flee
             Break my chains with haste
    And test my legs' strength,
             As I stampede like a wild steed
    A Stallion even
             Shiny, black
    Through my jungle of streetlights,
             Cars with horns roaring
    Like rhinos roughing road—

3-story apartment houses
To skyscraping projects
Towering over me like brick oak trees
Claustrophobing my mind
Walls caging in my ambition—

    Bullets gliding through air
    With swiftness to challenge any hawk
    Seeking to slay its prey
    Or blind flight like a bat in daylight
    Minus its radar sight
    Smashing into innocent flesh—

        Born and raised here
        Doesn't mean I belong here
        Or must stay here
        To mingle with jackals, hyenas, snakes
        Sneaky, two-faced
        Dwelling or living in front corner stores
        Seeking to scavenge a hustle
        Maiming minds with highs—

Trying to kill to live
Can kill a good's will to live
Force a heart to animalize

In order to survive
Amongst the fittest,
I must continue my gallop
Before this jungle swallows me up—

Environment man-made
Manufactured and maintained
By king of all beast
Roaring with degradation
Ordered jungle life regulation
With third-rate food
And alcoholic fluid as life-sustaining tools
While enforcers in blue
Hunt with hunger to use
And abuse power
Get their kicks from devouring
Meat of manhood
Humiliate to feel good
Itching to push one to attack
So they can react
With multiple warning shots in back—

    I must hoof it
    My locked mane floating behind
    As I dodge street posts lined
    Like thick vines
    Worn with erosion
    Trampling asphalt passing
    Fenced and gated pieces of
    Shielded property
    Marked for privacy
    Or each's safety from each other,
    Neighboring strangers—

        Here I don't belong
        Eyes long for serene seas,
        Wind waving misty breezes
        Like cool warmth,
        Removing shoes from heel
        Bruised and abused
        By harsh jungle grounds
        Now soothed

Ka-Son Reeves

                By sand crystals
Grains
                Massaged between toes
Easing my brain
                Stressed
From mentally tense
                Physically strenuous
Movements,
                Learned for survival
For now just wanna dive into
                Tranquility,
Jungle walls removed from me,
                Just lay back and breathe
My jungle a dream
                No longer seeking free
Awaken mind with tight eyes and
                Exhale
I am free.

JUST 1NCE ON THE 2

While trekking through Ghetto
Underground 2, just can't let go
Of the pain in my mental dwelling
Hence the strain, the constant swelling
Of the pulsing vein inside
Remembrance of when Boobie died
While straphanging her last ride
Kid is crying, gotta leak
Mama walk him to relief
Between cars, hold them bars–
Baby little-booty flashing
Straphanger's hands covering the laughing–
Little ruffneck rudeboys enter
Checking car inhabitants
Scanning round to see if safe
To act out—their soft hardness
As long as REAL ones aren't present
To slap 'em back to their right sense
Left, with their rehearsed utterances
Of angered ignorance
And exaggerated loudness–
Now they look at me
for an approval response
But I sigh
Because despite the act they still can't hide
Their pussy cat presence
Proved true once real ruff kats walked through
Shutting these kittens up quick
With an "I should jack you..." screw
–type face seems to, these felines, fix
I laugh to myself now... because
I thought I heard a meow
For mommy's nip-tip of
Security—it's simple
To simply act hard
But BEING hard comes with scars of built up pain
Physically trying to hide what haunts inside the brain
Embedded in face
That you can't fake and flaunt

Because eventually all masks come off—
Trekking through Ghetto is my plea for understanding
That we all have significance in this world of
Tests
We Learn to
Live
I lost a friend I used to dis
For his style, profile difference
Lavell braved the shame
Experience, I see the same, in a different way
In a society promoting what is not in me
Materialism and revelry rolling eyes at me
But fuck the haters, they can dis me yo
She already tap danced my ego
With him–
Man fuck 'em both I guess
Tssssssssss
Nah I don't mean that, that's just the
Stress within my chest
Some other pain
Open like prostituted lips portray
How I got fucked and cast away
Those are my thighs Florida
I was the first
Damn the best love
The first one's an eternal curse—
WHOAAAAAAAA!!!!
Thought's distracted
By train's sudden shift in speed
Rocking me to right
Screeches dance a flicker with light
Heightening the beat
Sudden fear of death
Already present in this environment
God
Now entering my life
With bright bull horning might
She's screaming
SAVIOR IN THE LORD
Above the screeching
Not what I had in mind, Aboard
A mobile church service?

"REPENT, JESUS LOVES YOU"

Now she's singing, no screaming church tunes
As she circulates
A paper-worn collection plate
For us to donate on train stay
Man I say no
Brochure she hands me
I say no
Evil she brands me
I say NO!
God sees my heart
And he sees yours too
So you better stop
Judgin' me, he's judgin' you
Sermon stops
She trots an attitude—
(wheewwwwwwwww)
Sit back an exhale to continue contemplate
Distracted by
    Rumblesandjolting

                and

                          screechingandhalting

    huffing heartbeats...

Oh–

    It's just my stop.

Ka-Son Reeves

NiGGER RiCH
(ANGRY CREDiT NiGGA)

My slavery is neo
I am a neo slave
Trapped within a moving cargo
packed for underground shipping to my destination
Wasting life with dough accumulation
For what
Mu-fucka can't reap his benefits
Each check, Mr. Bill come take his 3/4 split
I guess that's what I get
For tryin' to live a rich life on credit
Ain't paid shit back now I owe beyond
My limit
Income tax brackets?
I'm in a bracket called "Nigger Rich"

Meaning

You makin' mad dough but you don't own shit
You can't buy a house 'cause you lived
"Nigger Rich"
You can't rent a crib 'cause you lived
"Nigger Rich"
Steady payin' out the ass on some finance charge stiff
Payin' interest instead of interest
Paying you from stock tips
Make steady ends
But can't sign a car in my name
'cause of fucked up credit

My shit was on point for a while
A grin of perfection face would boast
Proud, disciplined,
Good credit specimen
Til overtake of ego—Greed now entered mind
Building tolerance of moderation
Man, fuck a future time
I WANT IT NOW

Everything seems to be on sale
Can't miss opportunity to own material world

            NO!

          Nevermind my limits
        Keep signing deeper hole
   Relying on that big future job to play my gold
           Pit gets deeper
           But it's aight
         The minimum I'll get
   Or pay just enough to keep a nigga
           Free to spend
            Addiction

I wanna stop the shop but cards keep calling me
To pop 'em in religiously
Dispensin' cash from ATM
But APR inflation makes it hard to balance pay equation
Tidalwavin' pockets bury me in owin-now absorbin' me
I make enough to feed a fam
But Chase lays out the biggest hand
Reminding me of credit spree
Ain't nuthin' comin' atcha free
Refuse to pay—
With penalty Chase slaps my face
Discover Card and HFC
is in the race
Prepare to slap my other cheek
I'm hurtin' broke
Pockets linty
Now I'm past due
Strugglin'
Bankruptcy, help me!!!

OF WEED AND WHITE POWDER

Each the reason behind each other's sorrows
Borrowing hate from each
Flaming like a torch passed around
to burn emotional scars deep into the grounds
of their inner esteem,
A village built on weed
and white powder walls
to float high with red eyes,
Sad and mad is the ness
Nest of unhappiness
River tears overflow dammed doors
Locked-in residents
Key of progression, escape
stays placed in hand
But mind's fear bans a try of a new eye
hoping to climb
above the weed and white powder walls,
So deeper in, they continue to fall—
Seeds are planted by accident in this village
Pilgrims of poverty move laterally
Expecting nothing from a new
something growing from the ravaged soil of a
mother's womb,
Doomed to die a failure
or a burdening anchor,
Their continuance in this existence
is in reliance of a coin toss,
Fifty to toss away, the other percent
preps your stay
in this planet hell
Heads or Tails—
Are we here because they
Won...
    ...or Loss
   the coin toss?
        hmmmm...
              ...I wonder.

SELF-INFLICTED SLAVE

I am a self-inflicted slave

It's 9am pass me my chains
Maybe they'll release me at 5 o'clock
But with all this passed down work,

maybe not

I can't escape, flee, seek them hills
For this slavery must pay my bills
What can I do, these beds I made

I am a self-inflicted slave.

Ka-Son Reeves

Civil Wars

How do we walk away
from a chain welded to our lineage
and a bricked world growing a fucked up existence,

                Ain't no pride to be made in a place
                that holds our hand backward
                and blinds our eyes with the fear
                that we should not step away from here,

Because out there will eat us up faster
and more inhumane than the shots we dodge
in street lanes and sidewalks
fit the scene like street lanes and sidewalks,

                Common as sense—

Where eighteen is the age where we
don't graduate and welcome the beginning
of higher education,

                But the new feeling of telling our mom to
                stay the hell out of our business,

While we bring our loves in
and test our sex in mom's bathroom—winds blow
faster because we have to show
we're old enough to create a new life,

                Though not smart enough to realize
        that it's hard to try to raise a baby in our bedroom—
                        babydolls
                never need to eat or absorb pampers,

And they sit on the shelf when we don't wanna play
or wanna play... out, but
we can't because of constant drama with our baby
daddies and mamas,

Many of us have parents who had us as teens
so that's education
with a lesson that
if we do pursue higher education and success
we're too good for this world
unless we're earning our success on street lanes and
sidewalks,

fitting the scene like street lanes and sidewalks,
If not, we need to get off or out
because we ain't representin' right
and we risk dying for our "I still belong here" fight,

Funny, that fight was fought before our country's war
was civil,
Now we're fighting self in new wars that are anything
but civil,

With the same pieces on both sides,
No human progression or pride,
and from the outside—

              Just
             A
           bunch
         of
       black
     animals
   killing
 each
other.

SICK

Sick of screaming car horns,
Trash talkers,
Double and triple parkers,
Broken elevators,
Pissy staircases,
Waterbug invaders
Dogs crapping on sidewalks
Uh... Pooper scooper?
Weed smoke by corner stores
Sick of kids saying that they I think I'm
all that
Just because I don't spend nights hustlin'
bags

Sick of friends phony,
  Fake,
    Double-faced snakes
      Sick of struggling for satisfaction
        First loves always asking
          My biz
            Entering and exiting heart
              Leaving lasting scars of harm

Sick of Strength testing,
Mind stretching sanity
Worrying over whether
Parental mental flexibility
Can handle worrying over me
When she's sick of worrying
Over me worrying
Over her worries...

Sick of paying for a hustle swindled into
  Being naive enough to get swindled into
    But I guess I must take credit for it
      At least that's how the collectors tell it
        Harassing my home
          Threatening by phone
            Job never to leave me alone

Sick of red signals
Congestion
100 stuffed in each
subway car section
Scratchy announcements
telling me
To be patient
While I'm the one getting fired
for my lateness

Sick of years of full-time night school
Saturday morning classrooms
To get a degree that's worth shit
Beause I lack field experience
To do the job school "trained" me to do
But if that's not enough
Then what's the point of school?

Sick of money lovers
luvvy duvvy green
trying to persuade me to
Share in love of
accumulation
Saying simple living's
misguided
Or misfitted,
Now I'm a social alien

Sick of loving what won't be
Liking what can't be
Wishing for the forbidden
Not accepting one's offering

Sick of pursuing fantasies
Repeating history
Not learning from misery

Sick of TRYING to be happy
When I just wanna BE happy without trying

Sick of pursuing what I don't know,
What is happiness?

    Sick of selflessness
    So I adapted
    selfishness
    But now sick of selfishness
    Beause natural is selflessness

Sick of writing with fear of reciting
 Introversion be my burden
  "Grab the mic man, you mad nice"
  "You could touch so many with your words"
   I know
    but fear
     attention stage glares
      causes nerves
       Until that's gotten over,
       I guess
        I'll be one of the nicest kats that you
        NEVER heard
       What a waste,

Sick of frontin'
Sick of masks
Sick of being pressured to complete a task
Sick of hours spent for parking places
Always taken
Found a spot way down a trot
too far walking
Cabbie pick me up man, come on, stop frontin'
Racist sumthin'

    Sick of racism of own
    Discrimination cause me
    To get passed over
    Or pulled over
    Got some nick bags in ya pocket?
    Nah Copper they at home
    With the crack and the poppers
    Heart stoppers
    Not true, but why a dude

Gotta crime life live
Because Brooklyn's the land of crooks
So I guess my residence fits your description
of a criminal's looks...

Sick of norms,
   Barriers,
      Born limit carriers
         Ten percent, don't use more than that
         If you do, trouble's on your back,

      Sick of searchin' for what I can't find
    Or finding what I'm not searching for
Sick of never having time

Nine hours at work, two hours to and fro
 on the 5 moving slow
  One hour morning, get ready
  One hour night, bed ready
   Seven hours more for sleepless nights
   My un-rested head
   Tell me. What's left?
    Four hours left to live each day but still
    I contemplate
    My thoughts are steadily spent
    Wondering where in the hell
    Has all the time went?
    Alarm rings my burning eyes
    Damn, is it a new day?
    But I haven't even slept yet
    Sick of living this way.

LOSiNG iT

Many times in mind
Both day and night dream time
Thoughts design fantasies
Alternate realities
Time still, but still moving fast
Like a relay race, but I'm running last
A dissatisfying taste
When ribbon of victory doesn't wrap around
My diligence
My best flushed into waste receptacle
A somber heart recycled
Reinvents into a winning experience
Excused as outlook positive
Hiding the crying of a sore tired strength
Caging the banging and beating
Kicking and screaming
Fits of frustration
Within my rib
A shaky smile pulled together
Flexing face to hold it better
So as to keep it sincere looking—
Never—
Can I reveal the weakening of a stone wall
Cracking a constipated smile
Like Uncle Bashim's gleam
As he five's me smooth and slick
Like his Superfly ponytail
Telling me everything's
Clean as green
I wish I could feel as serene as my
Uncle Bashim

                          seems,

                                      Hmmm

                                                  Seems...

PHONY HOMIE (REVISITED)

        Why be phony, homie
     Front me like the old school buddies

"What's up?"
    "How you doin' yo?"
        "This here is my bro."

Declaring love of a shoulder-companion
To, all of my interests, claim to be having;

  Observing while on me you wrapped your
  arm
  A furtive motive in a fisted palm
  And constant smothering, huffed an alarm
  Investigate now past an eyelid's charm;

    To find revealed the truth you hid
    Of drafts on how to be this kid
    The documents displayed date back
    To when I gave first pound, In fact
    When looking back one can now see
    A presence befriending suspiciously;

      You latched to me, I felt your pull
      But didn't vision past your wool
      Facade, you fleeced and flimflammed-me
      Sheepheaded momentarily
      Enough to let protection down
      Like eyelids, let the double-cross abound;

        In time the labor of persistence
        Borne a suspected "Ka-Son Thesis"
        Complete with quotes, footnotes, goal
        be- for
        You to act this "Ka-Sonology"
        Success you find in performing me
        'Cause now you strut a silent mirroring;

Distorted though, your insight lacking
Foundation of true friendship-backing
Exposing you a caricature
Precise in plan but poor in picture
So flee you fabricated phony
You've been uncloaked, no longer my homie.

MY MIND IS FLUSTERED

Tired is my might...
        juggling..
        struggling..
trying to make sense of every emotion that so
swiftly creeps up and surprises;

Where do they come from?
    Where do they hide?
        Emotions grabbing hold, like a thief– all of
        a sudden,
            in your face,
                demanding attention,
            grabbing your jacket,
        even waving a gun in your face,
stealing the wallet of your mental capacity...
which is full of all the personal sentiments and logic
that makes sense of every day life

    Once taken— over —you feel robbed, vulnerable,
    thinking of nothing but of how to make thing
    normal again;

Fists forced to emerge in a stance
Arms splurge a flurry to fight off the mind-thief
ducking and dodging, swinging and bobbing
in this boxing match
        Feet latched to flat surface
            as i stand my ground with purpose
            to protect my faculties,
        They think they got me;

    Ouch, yes they caught me once, and twice
        but no third charm, my arm is blocking
        plus my neck cocked back
    I won't fall back
    But still I can't help but to think back
    to why they are fighting me
    where'd they come from originally?
    I must re-visit my memory...

From where have they emerged?
At some point in time, were these emotions learned?
Or dormant until a sharp disturbance awakened them?
Like heart blasts...
Bursting light on weak eyes accustomed to black bliss
and in retaliation they sought to illuminate this...
black... bliss;
Dig deep, even deeper...
Search the archives of the dusty passages to that
labyrinth of memory
Perhaps somewhere lying there will be... a clue
to the ravaging waves of relentless emotions
now taking control of you...
I mean me;

>With the illuminated eye I search through my maze-
mind
to find the source of my mental/emotional bind
Step under cobwebs, and a couple of skeletons
in dimmed darkness, though the aura keeps me curious
Eyes notice a door, labeled "memory"
I trip over bones trying to re-discover me
An open door and a dropped jaw
amazed by the maze
of a mind that's confusion-crazed
Look back at door
now reading,
"enter if you dare!
And if you get lost
you'll forever dwell here!"

"Here" is the past—
with stories that never seemed to end
Chapters left open and behind
with twists and turns to keep the mind
in constant wonder of maybes and mights

>But...

A decision must be made,
To continue searching for the answer
and risk being caught up in the valley of imagination
where memories long since forgotten, dwell
or to slam the heavy door of that time's eye shut
and lock the memories associated with it up;
No longer being able to feel it so deeply
But freed from the invasion of those strong emotions creeping
heavily make the heart drag with every beat—

                                       Eyes blur back and forth
                                  as head spins left and right
                                  looking for the right decision
                                Wishing it can be made for him
I mean I

                              But another mistake that would make
                                   if the decision of his life
                                       of mean my—
                         was left for someone else to make

Should I search for the source of my anger and pain
Or should I look forward, forgetting the source
But focus on changing from this point
My course
But the source may help piece the present together
providing the why, so that I can know better
So as not to repeat
that why— repeat
But if there is no why, search would be for wild geese
but what if forward forgetting
proves impossible to achieve
The longing will forever burn my heart's present scene
Or maybe start the recreation of a new heart
A new life, A new love;

                                    Eyes tighten, then tears
                                  sad dripping for seconds
                                  then opens with confirmation
                                        I nod his head
I have made a decision.

CHAPTER VI

AS THE RAINS FROM HIS SKY POURED

He stopped short of the stairs where she sat
still as a boulder, eroded and wet
from the rains her sky poured...

he stood short of the stairs where she sat
not wanting to get wet as the water still fell
on her
like a blanket, and his dryness was comforting
to him
and he knew it was wrong to watch,

but he stood creased and clean
short of the stairs where she sat
muddied now as their roof poured a waterfall
of dirt onto her;
he thought of the many downpours that pierced his
back
once upon a time
and shivers vibrated from his chest
a coldness that made him cough
and his nose moisten with water
and blood
—and these are just from
the remembrances!

so he backed up away
from the stairs where she sat
in fear as she fell to her knees
drowning her breath but moving on, not
—why is she enduring, he thought?
he would surely have run than face the deluge
she must be mad, as on her knees she stayed
hands clasped, mouth moving in silence...

the showers soaking the stairs where she knelt
sweated his forehead as he was confused about
what to do
he worked so hard to clean and crease
himself
himself—
I don't think you understand, I worked so
hard to dry myself
creased and cleaned he thought
but now she's laying flat on the ground
and he couldn't watch anymore
he ran out with his jacket into the pour
and as his jacket reached out, she got up
with the speed of a cat
on her feet with strength full,

and the rain suddenly ceased...
she took the jacket with care,
and gently turned him around still shocked
at her switch
she placed the jacket on his back
as the sun's light appeared as suddenly
as the rain departed;
her next move was with a dancer's grace
she led him a half spin face to face
and caressed his cheek before she floated away
with a smile and the rays of the sun giving chase,

and he stood there watching
on the stairs that she left
with her smile and her sun and her dancer's grace
—as the rains from his sky poured.

THE BEST THING I NEVER HAD

A wide silent grin faces me
Twinkle of a dreamy daze
Like New Naivety
Or maybe like a pair of shining explorers
Clad in round camouflage brown
Trekking a trail
Discovery into the mind of a mirrored gaze
Seeing that treasured thought buried deep beneath a
Stilled face;

Floating through flashes of fond memories
Privately sharing public seats
Squeezing lifetimes into maybe
Five or ten seemingly seconds of
Blurred movements
Still tongues but roaming thoughts...
Conversations carefully picked from mind's storage of
Preset inquiries
Hoping to get the most effective connection
From those five or ten seconds;

Nah, we just friends,
But keep searching my beautiful brown, shining pair of
intrigue
It's only platonic the way my embrace secures you
My hand cherishes you
My passion loves through you
Filling you with my heart's lying mind
But you're filling me
With the best thing I never had;

I have to think protectively
To not involve the magnetic charge
Pulsing within
Pulling me in like dry desert quicksand
Sinking my emotions
Into a beating black hole
Held in unknown trenches of weakness

Squeezing my shield of insensitivity
To repel feelings of attraction
Torn between freedom to play and flee them to pray;

Am I such a bad guy?
Finding highs in feminine love cries
Am I to suppress my person?
Her crying sun rained on my clouded ego
Told me to stop acting, or stop being
Smooth, sweet, sweeping feet of friendly hearts
While spreading my dust of disillusion;

Me holding their parts while they hold
Only hopes
That the burning pains of my "No"-s
Would stop being scribbled into their beating chest
While I pen my "Yes"-s on their hips, lips and breasts
Physically focused but emotionally blurred
Don't know what my heart wants
But I know what my blood yearns;

To flow stiffly, swiftly through physical freedom
Like a hawk
Released from its cage of emotional responsibility
But instead
Forced from the stage of a relationship play
No longer wanting my acts of love
All that I've been trained
So to keep up my sanity
I no longer dare to perform my heart there
For fear of further unappreciated tears
    and jeers
    and sneers
    and "of your love, I don't care"-s;

So a stone mask hides a mushy beat
Premiering a new drama called
"that wannabe player"
staring me
and those
my beautiful brown, shining pair of intrigue
are the treasure thoughts that you seek.

FERTILE SOILS

    End result seen many times as beauty
    As morning sunrise bright and red
    Like new batches of blossoming rosebuds
    But none were mine; I was never ready—

As I tread carefully through fertile soils
Carrying plentiful seeds of me
In hand without the safety of a bag
To prevent spillage
My grip, that of a bear,

        But a seed still drops here and there;

    As I carefully tread through fertile soils
    Feet wet with pleasurable moistness
    It feels blissful to stay in this
    Fertile soil smooth like oil against my skins
    And a seed drops here and there, and there again
    Even as I grip
    But I must tread on; I'm still not ready
    To bury a handful and cultivate,

        I must tread on;

As I carefully tread through fertile soils
Feet dancing in satisfying wetness
A back-glanced eye fixes a gaze
On path of past and I wonder
Through all of the bushes I have traveled
And all of the seeds that I've dropped
Why not have a legacy of trees sprouted
From my soiled footprints like mini-me's
To let me see, if even by accident,
Growth can exist,

        And I question;

    The fertile soils I carefully tread
    Lack production in their genetic thread
    Or seeds were numbered

Less than what a planting found sufficient
Or maybe seeds I carried were inefficient
To sprout;

Or maybe I was divinely helped enough to keep me free
From rooting self deeper in responsibility
Because He knows I am not ready,

                Since still, I have no buds;

And worry is crept from chest to head
As soils from past are sprouting
Other off-springtime babies just after I left
The land with seeds in hand that are dropping
Here and there,

                And still, I have no buds;

As I carelessly tread through fertile soils
Hands now open and raised with empty freedom
Relying on pattern of footstep walk
With no trail of new growth
Convinced seeds were worth a sterile stale
So I dance all my seeds worry-free
In raw earth,

                Knowing steps are to no avail;

Stressing the soils I carelessly tread
To dramatic pains and tears shed
Instead of cultivating the flower-bed
I stomp and dance with a selfish head;

Until my sole is pricked and I look
At my soil's red drippings
Blended with brown fertility
Traces of a sprout reaching out and over
Slumped into a fetal hump
And my soul is pricked as eye water falls
On fertile soil,

                And now, I've lost my bud.

MAUVE SKY

...pulled down the cloud high
and dyed its white cotton to match the sky's mood,
Mauve is its blues
Now the cloud is a fog bitter and opaque and heavy
And angrily runs through the horizon
to block out all the beauty of the city night's line;
The trees outside my window
that give me a bit of nature before the beauty of the city
try to duck out of the fog's way
as he speeds off angry and mauve—
Trees black and pointing 45 degrees
and I'm here feeling somber and sexual
but not necessarily sexy;
I barely brushed my teeth today and it's an hour to midnight
and my baby's flicking channels on the remote in a room far far away
and I'm not flicking her,
But flicking the keys on this computer screen facing
away from the drama
I'm witnessing outside—
    A storm that has the cat crying,
    Or a cat that has the storm crying,
    Or a pussycat that has my loins crying,
    Or my loins not having the pussy crying;

But rather sitting and writing about the deepening
mauve
now purple sky blues
from my window;
Violent and moving and screeching and flashing white
lightning
howling strong moan of thunder on an angry air
and from the inside of my window, a calm silence;
I see the mirroring effect my silent and empty room
casts
on the violent view of black trees and purple skies
clearing up slowly now,
and I could see the skyline soon revealed
and it's getting silent and calm,

        And I hear footsteps coming my way.

LEAN ON

So it was that he cried
finally couldn't hide
anymore, the lines tore
through the wall inside;

Mama told him to listen
to the ails of the other
papa told him to control
the emotional smother;

But mama he lived with
pop was just weekends
the teachings he'd plead
the effects were just weakened;

So he was mama's boy
the woman's ear
not the womanizer
he welcomed the tears;

The shoulders, pop's muscular
work-outs were seen on
became more effective
for a woman to lean on;

And lean on, and lean on
soon they would cling on
the shoulder, whip-cracking
demands they were seen on—

And he'd obey
you can say
spoiling his women
is what made him that way;
He saw his mama struggle–
to care for a woman
is why he strengthened
his shoulder's muscle;

And pops wasn't there
no matter how much
his presence appeared
it just wasn't enough;

Mama's influence
dominated his state
not just her teachings
but his view of her way;

Of life–
fending for herself, one might
conclude that his cope
was to help bring hope;

To another–
making queens of women
who deserved it would help
make it up to his mother;

But they'd lean on, and lean on
soon they would cling on
the shoulder, whip-cracking
demands they were seen on—

Mama told him to listen
to the ails of the other
papa told him to control
the emotional smother;

But
nobody told him how—
to balance it all
so look at him now;

The women he chooses, demand his attention
marking, off limits, their prized possession
a relentless scold if he misses a step in
pleasing his queen, and I don't mean in sexing;

More like the grapes of wrath–

and the feather-fanning
winds of ache in his wrists
fuels a frustrated path;

So it was that he cried
finally couldn't hide
anymore, the lines tore
through the wall inside;

And out poured a ferocious beating
ending in flying feathers floating
and grapes smashed so fine
they can pass for wine;

And a deserving queen, no longer gloating
but spitting out feathers
and wiping off grapes and wine from her eyes
to stare at her shoulder walking away,

And simply asking, but why?

A WOMAN'S BEST FRIEND

She said her eye caught sight of me
And that was it...
Because it didn't seem profound enough
To mend the split...
Hindering her decision
To walk the talk
So she made herself at home atop that famous fence
While I, "the dog", who purchased my own chain and leash
Held the end and said,

You can own me...
If you just take two steps away from
where your misery lay burdens
I'll take them and bury them with my bones
And I'll walk with you through new strolls
My bark is a soothing whisper
Sweet and soft
My bite is a massaging nibble
A chill-inducer
That pumps goose bumps in lines down tingling skin
Toward the sensitive tissues within
Escaping through fleshy perspiration
—I purr kittens baby
My growl teases better than it sets off fear
So the feline attraction will want to be near,

A woman's best friend—

But she keeps asking "Why?"
When I tell her I'm drawn to the light in her eyes
She said with those eyes she can't perceive
Why I get weak when I stare
At her — still atop the fence;

Believe me, she emits instinct in me
To caress and squeeze and tease and please
Oh please she brings out the dog in me!
Not the way dogs play out similies

Of humps and pokes on anything
But the immediacy of loyalty, man
For her I huff and pant and sit
and stay and tilt my head in that angled way
Like "Urmph..."
My restriction on lust is officially stray;

She loves my compliments
I know
Because she asks for more with her lashes
Buzzing me like hummingbirds
I heard the whispers of her eyelid's words
"Make love to my mind...
Make my intellect wet...
Stimulate my brain with the most passionate SEX-ual
type experience—
And watch my skin no longer hold in
The heat and moisture building within...
Do you have handy, a napkin?"

—But still, she sits on the fence;

Hence my hold is growing cold
My lease's rejection is blatant and bold
Insulting even
And I wonder why, but then realize
My offer's on the side of the fence
That she left...
She opened her hand and it all came back
When I saw what that hand held,
Bright and red
And instinct barks and pants and jumps with excitement
Look, it's my play toy!
Still partially shredded from my puppy days
Of fun and games
Oh I loved the squeaks my play toy made;

She tossed it to me and my jaws locked tight
And I caught it... boy, oh boy,
I shook my head with violent joy
And bit and pulled and bit again
Rolling around with great enjoyment

Till I felt it thump...

> I stopped and dropped and stared as it
> Thumped once more, then lay silent
> I picked it up and brought it back
> To her atop that fence
> Only she wasn't there
> She was back on the other side
> Walking
> I dropped my red toy and stared
> At her back
> From behind the fence,
> Her head seemed to not be there,
> It hung so low;
>
> I huffed and panted and sat
> And stayed
> Tilting my head in that angled way...

Like "Urmph."

NO I'M NOT

My tap sparked a swift turn
in my direction, her stare burned
like a stick of scented wax, her
aromatic heat flapped its wings
upward into the two towering tunnels
extruding from a countenance seeking
an expression
to permanently call its own,

Remember that look called a smile?
that reared itself once in awhile
like after a baby burp
innocent
or a lovebird's chirp
melodious,

But my reticence was cold
and formal to those burning eyes
and I felt the flame dissipate
as she blinked and turned away
with a motion slowed down for me
to catch up to the game
lustful genders play,
that sensual tease
and I want to play
but I do take my time
too much to say,

"I don't know why I wave goodbye
when opportunities pass my way...
I am bluntly afraid of failure
and even more terrified of success
leading to the land of happiness...
so thanks for stopping by,
I wish you the best
the mess I made
is my bed, and here, alone I will lay
it has been comfortable lately"

Before she turned a final time
she took her scent with her and said...
"You, muthafucka are crazy!"

DOME PLUCKIN'

For years...

Self's pity took up residence
in an open mind and shut its doors
so that no one else may enter

    to disturb the workings within its occupancy
    and the changes it hoped to make
    and had made immediately

        after its security was shattered–
        like an esteem battered it fled into that
        inner hiding place
        disgraced by an ego who had given up his
        cape
        no longer super–
        Supreme his being, trampled
        leaning as he walked for support
        see he couldn't stand straight
        His esteem was held low and heavy
        swaying like a pendulum
        hypnotizing his state;

Look into his eyes
and watch your heart beat
burgundy cries
He struggled to shake the daze
like dice gambling in permanence
he became amazed
because willingness to take this risk
was already in a bit, a lift
And strength entered his fist
in whispered words of encouragement
by a rose brushing his ear sweet
like her nectar meat
(damn too steep in vulgarities);

More like a petal
   Door to a black hole filled with light
shining a likeness of his darkness
         but with insight,
And it felt right
   to be a dark light
She called him a dark knight
   flying with mended wings
with holes that whistled in the breeze
   he used to land his manhood on his feet
but now he scrapes his knees;

                 His confident strut is now contrived
                    to keep that image in the eyes
               of those who think his nonchalance
                         is a natural prize–
                      Not knowing it's a disguise–
           he wears shades to hide the remnants
                  of his many years of cries
               pain from many found out lies
                he even cries from the lies
                he hasn't found out yet
because the pain consumed and hid, makes him suspect
                 that everyone's out for blood...

In this hole
he saw himself as all of this
but in viewing, no tear left his lid
this time
he just closed his eyes
and turned away to say the lie
was easier to keep...
She told him it's not easy but the truth is a relief
away he kept his eyes
his strength was spent to keep it steady
she closed her petal and her hole
and said, "you are not ready."

CHAPTER VII

SUNRISE CAPTURING

In a sunrise
a cool, silent darkness
slowly blends into brightness;
cool winds transitions into warm breezes
eye opening beginnings,
colorful rays of a new start,
shiny yellow orange awakenings,
energetic yawns, contracting inhales
followed by relaxing exhales,
refreshing smells of anew;
then freeze right there and capture that moment like a snapshot
placed in memory
except frozen movement still motions continuously smooth,
  forever feeling the bliss of a sunshiny kiss of sun's rays
                      against
                        face
                        cheek
                        and lips,
reflecting shine back to sun through the puckering of
warm innocence;
receiving giving receiving giving
you sun you sun
forever you and sun together becoming one
sunrise froze in time,

the world moving on
but minds on same timeline,
keeping sunrise in eye
carrying captured coalescence,
a glow seen by passers-by
Often summed up by letters L-O-V-E
But I guess it's just that rare case
of sunrise capturing.

KISSING THE SUN

Every sunray that touches me
reminds me of the warmth of your hand
and I have no choice but to turn around
and return a smile
to the sun,
my sun...
Have you ever blown kisses at the sun?
Have you ever gave chase toward the sunray's run?
Have you ever had swift sudden feels of blown kisses
tapping at your cheek?
That's me
guiding with deep wishing as they're gliding upward
toward the sky like pale pink butterflies
ending their existence
as they pucker and disappear in the distance
on the lips of my sun;
Feeling complete as their purpose is now done;
Time to send another one.

AT A GLANCE

The lids that blinked heart beats of life
Given early then taken late in youth
Paused wide to let a teary eye dry
Long enough for love's pupil to shrink in focus
Like an automatic shutter anxious to snap
She shot a single signal with her twinkle
A blinding light into the unknown
As she floated in a motion slow as a moment
That lasted my time's life
And flashed years before this lid's eye
As paradise played out in my imaginative memories
Not yet made
But longed
And without blinking
Eye listened.

EPISODE II

Creamy smooth alpine curve waist

Downward stare

Contouring hips with fingertips
Her bitten lip
My vision trip

Long strands of honey auburn silk
Blends away slight her gaze

Her moaning eye
Catches I
As I
Slide tips softly
Down side of thigh

Heads down but
Eyes fixed
On lustful opposites

Caramel and chocolate
Aphrodisi-sweets to mix

Hungry minds, erotic slys
Clever tries, successful kinds

Eye observing, body curving
Bed
The whirlwind
Passion turning heads

Spinning, wet lands

Lost control of subtle roles
The primal mode
Organic stroke
Orgasmic grope
Climactic hope

Acquiescence–

Chin hooking shoulder blade
Pressed firm holding place
With arms strapping upper back
Squeeze torso with flexed leg-wrap
And clamp
To hold bodies steady
As we rhythm movement plenty

Thrusting breaths
clear beads of sweat
glistening streams
from face to chest

erecting depth of push

cushioning couple
round and supple
tongue twist a lick
tooth pick a nipple
nibble stiff

swift is the way to the bliss
we play like cubs on green
tropical jungle
screams
SCREAMS
SCREEEEAMS!!!!

eeeeease into satisfaction
as I chase my breath with a net catching portions
and smiling because she's smirking with her own net
and just a few more breaths.

CAVE WOMAN

Who cares if like a bear
A woman steps aggressive and sincere
To demand the satisfaction
Of some energetic action
Call her Cave Woman
Grab your man's hair and then pull him
To your cave with animalism
Make HIM scream YOUR name then kick him
Out the door and have your snore
With the pride of a slutty whore,

And tomorrow, ya just might call for some more.

STRUMMIN' MY GUITAR

"Hey, over here, get off that
computer and play with me...so what
you'll get in trouble, just stroke me,
just a little, I'll sing if you do..."

Gazing at its smooth, curvaceous, glistening figure
caressing her vocal cords for a moaning note
from her rounded, opened mouth...
finger tips sliding up and down her long, slender neck,
massaging slowly then quickly
as I'm holding securely, almost gripping
swiftly up and down
as she screams melodic sounds
enticing me to brush strings
creating songs from her inner being...
spread across a kneeled lap
forever posed in acquiescence
body, mine to play with
    under my control,
    whether wild or tamed pick–
    use many moods when I'm caressing
    multiple tunes through her I'm expressing
we're shiny things
she's moving with me
a lap dance in sync
tickling her fast and slow
as her moan continues to grow
ringing pleasant things
in an ear at attention
to twine with body extension
groping and stroking
her hard body, fluid motion
we move, we ocean
wearing my beads of streaming sweat
I press as she lets out a final pleasure cry
pulsating against my palms I close my eye
and breathe and release her most sensitive string
as she lies down next to me...
                                ...her moan
fading.

RESPONSE TO A PAINTING

Difficulty to see through screens
  And lines in between
    Of what one really means
      To one;

    Eyes met with a painting
  Beautiful
   Saw before
But never took time or
Had enough courage
   To look past the instant
      Attraction
         But now looking closer
            And with a little more maturity
         Realizing an appreciation
      So with newer eyes
    He takes his time
To analyze the focus of his admiration;

He's an artist as well
    So with critical eye
       And intrigue her canvas he touches
          Eye closes—
             Back holding he tries
                To hide his heart and mind's cries
             Out to the artist to step from behind
          The painting to reveal the hand behind the art
    To show him some more of what was revealed
Hidden messages of passion
But of more that's concealed;

     We all have faults
     Imperfect strokes and deep thoughts
     Colored moods
            Lays a hand of understanding
            True acceptance he's branded
            Know that though sloppy and stained
                 Artistic colors nonetheless;

For dry and cracked paint
He wishes to add
His liquid of love
Watercolors—
Colorfully flowing
Deep inside of their breasts;

That's what makes the beauty
That his heart yearns to touch
For in time his heart's find
Was an artist caring and kind
Generous and sensitive
Well-defined mind
To hear more and feel more
From the artist he adores;

For now he wishes to step
Inside of the painting
To learn her true thoughts,
True feelings, true faults
To share shyly his many
Wants not be ashamed, but be accepting
Then maybe together leave the painting
Her lovely hand placed in his
To enter a new canvas of life
Sharing a painted love
Brushes mixed
Two imperfect brushes one fine stroke
Expressing a love only one hopes;

But he opens eyes
Tear flows from face
Maybe in another canvas
Another place
Know, she would
In love, fell, he with her
Explain he could, of its spark;

But instead fingertips he kisses
And on her canvas he presses
        And wishes to one day meet the real artist
        And tell her, she has
   Of him,

        Already pleased

        And satisfied.

CHAPTER VIII

IT MUST MEAN I'M FALLING... AGAIN

Like a cloud, I float weightless over earth
Held up by her heart's whisper
A breeze of security, under me
Navigating through her innocence
I suspend time and I
Long enough to wonder why
Like a dream I sleep in fantasy
Inside of her reality
Afraid to Awaken
Ears covered by palms to silence
The hypnotic chimes of her beats

thump thump... thump thump...

Yet they're soothing me
Lifting me up above
Hollow ground from which I came
To accept as my domain
Placed by a pained first
She revived me with a burst
Of winded kisses
Eyes closed in mediation, deep down

I really want to listen.

FROM A MEADOW FROLIC - PART II

I want to take your hand
    and let it blend in my palm as my arm gets strong to
lift you
    high above mine and your ground
hear the sound of the sky sing in our ears
    like la-la-la-la-la—
You and I are the
    ones who the soul has meshed beneath the bone
we're flying through a love zone;
    You ever see the redness of the finest clear sunsets?
The ones that bend the rays of light
    in color shining bright and shaded
a couple laying down in grass greener than the wealth
    their eyes see when they pluck
images of mythical love stories,
    and they draw out with their fingertips a guy and girl
connecting lips?
    That's us;
A swirling sunset romancing the minds
    of those who wished they were in the sky
like us...

CARESSING A ROSE

Prickly–
On the side of bitter even
And I have walked away with many scratches and scars
From trying to hold its stem as I sniffed
Or trying to lift it out of its home
Thinking my samaritanism is at work
Or even selfishness
Me and my posie
Dreams of fitting it in a pot that I will buy
One that will finally get its attention
To see that my home is better than the bitter grounds of
our youth
From it, how can we grow?
That's why I moved.

HOW WOULD I HAVE DANCED?

Well, I would have pulled a closer ear
to better my movement in touch with yours;
I would have panted less, breathed freely more
With our torsos pressed, body listening
to make our pair a more passionate mesh;
Gazes would have been reciprocated
deep beyond the chocolate pearls
into the essence of a deeper message;
Heartbeats would have drummed
to the exhaling pulses of
     our senses...
And then we'd start...

          Dominating the desire
             for now I see the fire
          tamed wildness is smiling
       my mildness replaced with readiness
        through bushes and branches
        overtaking natural madness
           movements unrehearsed
     speed rising–wind rising
               dust flying;
        minds fixed on grips of each
     opposites
         in intertwining bliss
   we are the forests!
    two now one dancing
 — swinging-twisting-romancing —
our verbal dance
  wild locks tamed fast
    head back in my comfort hands
      security with sweet
         me lifting your feet
     for the lyrical sweep
   holding your air beneath
    no more fear-wiping sweat;
        — crowd applauds —
           Now that's a dance there!

"HIS PLEA OF DIFFERENCE"

Watch the artificial sunlight from the bricked sky
Shine on my blackness
Although I'm pale brown in spring
Red in summer
Beige in winter
I whisper into the microphone things like my flow is seasonal
Colorful not just in hue but in inner's description of me
Call my self a rainbow
Rainbow man!
Beyond the current trend of connotations
My description digs for truer and more enduring senses
In my eye a rainbow is not a bow but goes past what your eye sees
It goes under and around and reflects the light of this earth in 360 degrees
You may find it hard to consider a rainbow
More than the arc that your ears tell your eyes to interpret
And even harder to hear it from a man unless he is sensitive and prances out
A feminine form
But it is ok…

I Am sensitive
And I prance *inside* toward the side of completion
To let the rainbow in me that shines 360 degrees move me toward that completion
Of a whole
Man—

So I will help you shop for your shoes, love
Watch you try them on and strut your sexuality toward and away from me
Buy them with you even
Then take you home and take them off of you
Slowly

And knead my energy through your toes with my fingers
To let you know that more than a machismo mask, it's the
Time
That's precious
And that we take...
                      It...
                                  slow...

Then I grab the microphone again
On this stage that is my confession booth and scream...

                I AM A SENSITIVE MAN!

  I WANT NOT YOUR BODY BUT YOUR THOUGHTS IN MY
                        HAND!

                I WANT TO LISTEN!

I WANT YOU TO FALL IN LOVE WITH THE LOVE THAT
               HAS FALLEN FOR YOU!

I just want you to see what makes me tick
That mushy red pulser that's become endangered out here;

And then I won't need to ask for your body
  Because it would be mine;
    And I would care for it as mine,
      Caress my breasts;
        Moisten my fingers with my lips,
        Spoil my skin with kisses
      That most macho men dismiss,
    That I know you miss;
  And you'll want to call yourself Mrs. _____
For whatever you say my name is.

I AM

        Standing on a flat surface
        Head bewildered as I glance
        At the span of plain space
        Waste,
        Unfamiliar land
        Empty,
        Except for spots of gleam
        Pushing through in between
        Cracks of concrete
        As she hands me
        A shovel and shoes
        Saying these are your tools
        Now dig;

With difficulty,
Shovel breaking, muscles hurting
Feet aching
As I try to grant her request
Slam with force and then press
In,
But not penetrating
As winds of desertion
Push against body exertion
Like resistance against my statue stance;

        I focus all my strength
        Arms raised with tightened might,
        Deep inhale–
    Whistling wind wrapping around skin
Trying to wrestle me from my position;

      One quick glance round motion
        Misery,
            Tumbleweeds roll with gusts
                Of barren blue blackness;

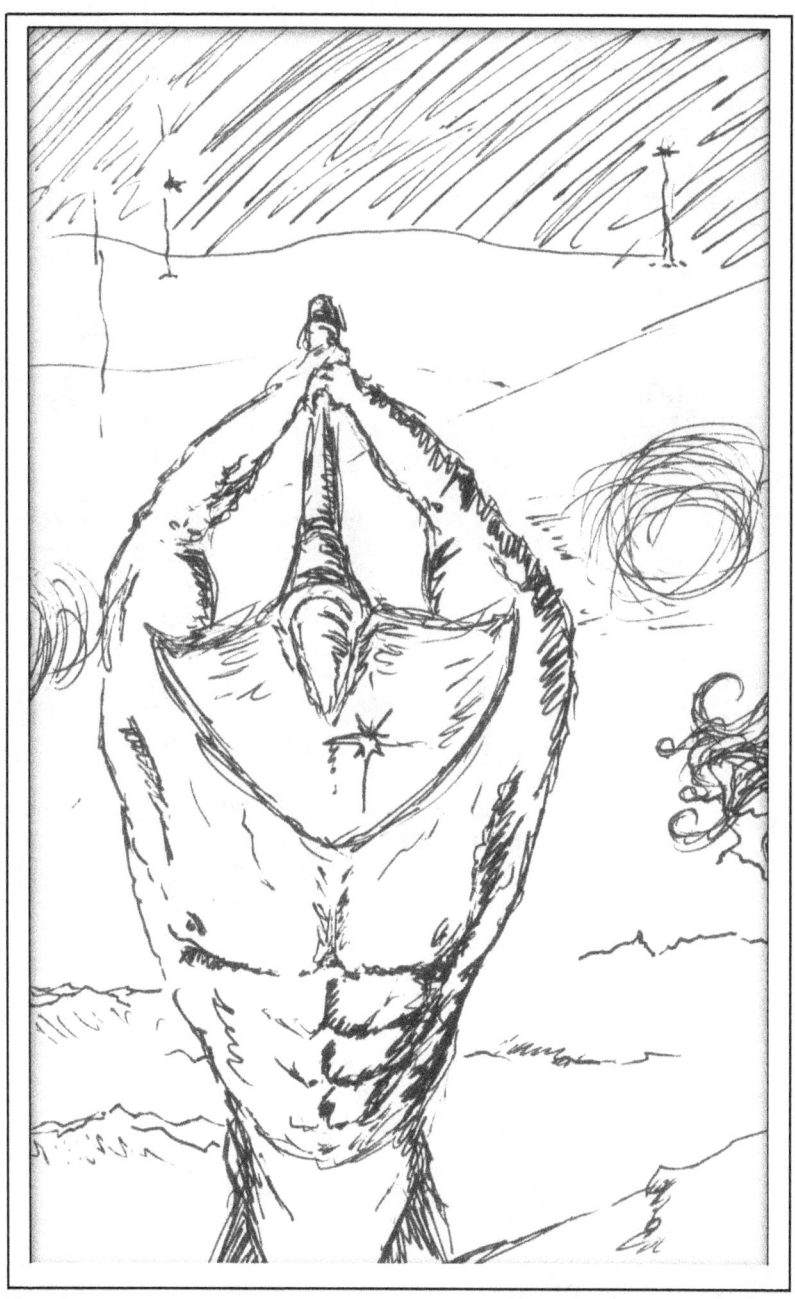

Eroded surface for miles
Her eyes squinted she smiles
You can do it...
She clutches fist as thin
Vein shoots up through her arm
Like a lifeline of might being transferred
Into me,
Like she's holding with me
Or maybe used to what I'm feeling currently,
Last strike, all strength
If this doesn't work, there's nothing left
ARGGGGGGGGG
STRIKE!
(psheewwwwwww)

                        Thin line of bright white ray
                           Strays upward straight
                           Like a powerful geyser
                                Force fell me,
                    Shaking my daze, I finally
                       Up raise and focus on ray
                    Brightening blue atmosphere
                      Immediate area at least
                                     Here—
Hand outstretched with intense shakiness
    Like trembling of a frightened curiosity
        Moves arm independent of reasoning
                             Slowly extending
       Eyes mesmerized by the hypnotic bright
                              Of rays light—

Crystalline sparkle
Golden stream fine optical dream-like
WOW...
Chilling vibrations shoot swift
Like a current of blissful promise
Feelings of strength, greatness
Completion, warmth, leadership
Security
Envelops me instantly

But...

    Just as quickly
        Shining light leaves me
            A hollow mood
                Like the raw energy of a potent battery
                Removed
                    A need to recharge
                      Sensation desire enlarging
                To semi-addiction
        So shovel again up I pick and
Pause;

For throbbing of aching muscles
    Remind me of its struggle
        To pierce surface,
            She looks at me as shovel falls
            Too heavy to hold,
                She smiles...
                      She thanks me for putting myself
                In her shoes
                  Seeing what she sees
                  Feeling what she feels
In me,
    For I am her unfamiliar land
        Her barren blue blackness
            I get it now...

I am her light.

CHAPTER IX

'CAUSE EVEN NOW, I'M AMAZED

Your eyes are pendulums of both love and desire
  Your smile shines a warmth on my skin
    Penetrating the beats that I count to coincide with the amount
      Of declarations you make and I take in
        To make me feel, special;
          I know I don't verbalize my emotional vibes
            But I hope this expression reaches your insides
          And you take it in so you can feel what I feel for you
        That you are to me, special;
      Mornings are nice to see risings of sun shine on your face
Embracing the covers that you squeeze and wrap around like
        A baby in peace's place;
         And tranquility makes me smile
           And laugh because your foot's sticking out
              Although you're neatly placed on YOUR side
            That foot shows you're still a bit of wild;
          Baby fingers and tiny toes
        Adds to the cuteness that makes me say awwww
      She is just too cute;

But when you don that robe with hints exposed
Before it falls to the flaunt of control
Of your body
Damn you MAKE it good, and ooooh
DAMN! you know how to move; (knuckles in mouth)
You carry your love like a rose petal basket
To spread to the world you contact and don't mask it
In fear...
Even when I shake my head and tease
You with utopian compares, you still make it clear
That it's only your self that you wear,
And not any false sheepish gear
Like the wolf...
I hope you know that all I need
Is to think of you and inspiration creeps
Into my description of inner beauty
Blossoming out to where everybody
sees;

Beauty actually starts with C.

A PRIMITIVE AND INGENIOUS TRAP

        This is a story of a woman who sought a mind
                Mapped like a labyrinth
              She tread hope on a fine line,
           With quiet and set careful steps
     Her breath soft and paced with calm regularity,
            Her eyes squinted and focused
                She kept control
          You see her role was that of docility,
Although her heart was trained to pound earthquakes
                  Of sensitivity
             Into the hardest of beats;

          I thought it was neat myself
  Because there I was unwittingly laying down plans of
                    falter,
And she just jumped jumped
Jumped off of and over those traps
Like a jackrabbit or track star without a time limit,
For her race winning
She sought her prize with patience;
And that pricked me you see
Because I was steady placing more tracks
To further complicate my mental maze,
I was told my enigma was self-induced
For the sake of being called enigmatic, who
was producing proof? I?
I thought my purpose was just
To lay more tracks to keep her away
To keep her from reaching me lovingly,
Through angles and curves she swerved
and glided softly to find my nerves,
Like a soldier;

She wouldn't listen to hints to turn around
And forsake the idea that she could change
Everything,
Found a reason to bind herself to her mission
Because the vision she saw was of legends—
Of Eves and Adams and leaves and matters of nature,
nude
She believed that truth was found in the love she grew
From my mind and tear water and her beaten seeds
And our
Regenerated earthen needs
To sniff a reincarnated tulip;

But all I could see was the need to sniff
The moistness of two inner lips
She noticed this and with ingenious wit
Communicated in vulva terms and clitoral twists
To get me to listen to the real message,
There is more to it than this
Her lips said
But I wasn't sure which ones...
So I listened to them all just to be sure
That I caught it... all;

Because the feelings began to sound good
And the sounds began to feel good
And the more I listened, the more I felt
And the more I wanted to feel and listen
And I gave her all I had in time and mind
To experience... more;

Hearing something about worked plans and
baited clit cages
But seeing her smile, framed in blurred borders
and bubble hearts
Was all that mattered.

FRiDAY

I wanna see her inner lips tingle like a vibration
Palm-pulses make her hips move to the sensation,
Pressing in till, through, the wetness drips
She's fantasizing that my hand is causing the bliss;

    She's in her chair, eyes closed, feeling an arm from behind
Against her breasts, sliding down the inner of her thighs,
Grinds the forearm like a pole, she knows she might be seen
    Caring for nothing, except holding in her scream;

Down goes her zipper... pop goes the button
The fingers creep inside... pants stop nothing,
Silk reached... no longer dry
But naturally soaked by her sultry insides;

    Arm is gripped tighter... she's feeling penetrated
    Her mood is feeling lighter... a high is generated,
    She doesn't care, she's up in the air, off her seat
    Her hump is swift, harder... no longer discreet;

The fingertips are circling quick, feel the nails
Scratching, pressing deeper in skin, before she yells,
Breath swells, a bodily tremor, overwhelms
My wet arm, slowly eased from hot realms;

    Of imagination,
She kissed it and thanked me for the nooky narration,
A soft click as the worn phone lay on its base
Astonishment lay on every co-worker's face;

As her co-workers stared at her stripped-off shy way

    She left her job screaming **"TGI Fuckin' Friday!"**

THE HOT SEAT

In the moistness of the morning
  My mind wanders into ways to make that word
    Energize my insides,
      I blink and think of the puckering of lips
    Placed sideways in between legs widened,
And welcoming
  And I'm floating
    Following the invitation
      Of a clit calling like a forefinger
        Leading me in,
      And I can see myself swimming through wet air
    Toward the rosy pink petal folds with the pheramonic aromas
    Pricking and tickling my torso,
      And she wonders how she can spray me
        Like it's the ninth potion
      Not knowing I'm longing to be bathed in it,
    Exercising my back strokes and her breast strokes
I feel I've reached because legs are locking me
  And pressing tightly as I push a pelvic thrust
    Among gushes and rushes of sweat,

        Push
            Push
                Pushing my best...

A TROPICAL STORM IN HEAT

Wavy strands wrap like silk strings around my mind
Trapping my focus toward a fueled sensuality
I don't know if it's her or me
But I want to pick those strings and hear more chimes
inside of my inner rhythm
Squeeze me tighter and secure my focus
My sweat racing like marbles down a steep slope;
I must have lost mine
Because I am crazy about this situation
And I do not know why;
Decade numbers my last remembrance of such a storm
Loving exotic and in love with erotic
Isn't even the center of this poem's topic,
Although it isn't quite much missing either
With the wind and raindrops cooling my love's
disbeliever
You know that temperamental organ that rationalizes
Experiences
And through its bout with trauma shuts down for a while
The value and validity of emotions;
Some say think too hard and it'll become so hot
It'll burn out and you just might lose it
But my heart feels forced
To test the range of my thoughts
'Cause its desire is too strong to refuse it.

HEARTBOUND

Your eyes bat breezes that I inhale for the imagery of pinks
and wet reds in sun-shower-sunsets wrapped around my eyes
Like a leading blindfold that my footsteps follow
To a float—

The finger motion, motioning for me to glide into
A virtual exercise in heartbeats and body-meets
Like sweetness that dries to a stick
Is how I find myself
Stuck to you...

Do you kind of get it?

Wet heat loosens a hold and allows for breathing room
Then becomes an addictive adhesive when parting winds cool
Keeping me in proximity of that next invitation
Of batted breezes and finger wave teases
To glide into another virtual exercise
Rubbing myself with your wet heat
floating again until the cooling binds.

MORE THAN JUST A COMPLIMENT

Your lips are like soft petals
your lashes fan the loins fired by your aura
your hair flows sweet scents of mouth-watering thoughts
into my inhales
and I exhale shivers
quivering with nervous excitement at the
anticipation of exhilaration
I'm steady placing palms together in prayerful hope
     of just one more whiff
     of your naturalness
kiss mami kiss kiss blow winged blow kisses around my
neck fixes
     stiff goosebumps all over my senses of touch
        taste
           touch
             wait
                I want to slide slow
                    a fingertip or earlobe
transmitting a physical code
    hinting for me to be the boss in your abode
       waving away the cold
          welcoming the warm
             analogy of your loveliness
                an evening beach calm.

MY VERBAL MASTERPIECE

(Sit with me and see what I see
When I see you, posing in front of me
Like my art's model)

        I'll draw my thoughts through my words
        In description of my potential masterpiece,

Your eyes cause my head to shake
Pendulum pearls "nice like mine"
Entrances me a love slave
To give to you the gift of my life chains,

        And I shake my daze to follow the direction
        Of your hair long and black like me, but
        Sweet smelling and seductively sexy,

You run your hands through it like you love it
Long and black and I wonder if you love it because
It's long and black...
Like me...
Sweet smelling and seductively sexy,

        And I smile as my voice continues to paint down
        To your lips soft and wet and warm and set on
        Mine and my mind through my ear when you say
        Those things that are only expressed in a whisper
        And I insist...
        I said I insist it's your breath
        That pumps the beat that's leading me
        To focus on continuing my masterpiece
        With my artist's thumb out like my lover's tongue,

I focus and salivate
In a room dimmed as evenings
With sun sleeping violet breezes
Dancing our sheer white curtains
Penetrating with a soft rainbow glow
To spotlight my love's curved sanctuaries,

And a golden ray to gleam the central field-bush
Initiating the argument with my lower self
That one pant-tug settles,

                      Eyes sleep to increase my awareness
                      The heart of my masterpiece—

Nudity sheds flesh to expose without distraction
Before me and not my penile pleasures
And I can't paint anymore
Because my lips widen to an oval,

    To blow out no speech...

LOVE IS FOREVER ETERNAL

A strand picked from time's band
Or a single grain from an hourglass' sand
Hands insight into one's
    L.I.F.E.
One's
                      Love Is Forever Eternal—

See me walk worlds
Eyes guided, gliding like brown butterflies
Toward a newborn horizon
Reflecting lines of life's
    Time,
Contemplate
                      Love Is Forever Eternal—

Like hip movements dancing a passionate polka
Costumed in sheets played on bedroom stage
suites
Or a pondering sit, atop mountain lifts
Arms stretched, inhaling sky blue reddishness,

Love stands forever
Love lives eternal
    As God
As one prays to give praise for one's spiritual
ways
Bears faith for infinite days
    Love as Life
Name passage down to keep legacies 'live,

She breathes
Pushing a laboring scream
Relief as new eyes
    Blink new bonds
        As new hearts
           Beat new songs of life,

                        Love Is Forever Eternal—

    Man and Wife,
                Love Is Forever Eternal—

Two sights blend one view
Through the vow, "I do"
Till sleep ends age, like last sets of rays
'Pon faces that gaze an escapism daze
Self,
                    Love Is Forever Eternal—

Inner wealth,
Found in brush strokes or thought quotes
    In poems
Zoned in a twilight expression
Action free from creative oppression
Love Is Forever Eternal, a lesson
Neglected from feeding the seedling direction,

                Innocence − Education = Ignorance

Hand-holding sweethearts of school
High view of fantasy
Future was stepped too soon to see
Life, reality
Bitterly splits the grip
Walk in teariness
Though, on, moved since
    Time
Still revealed through eyes for life,
                Love Is Forever Eternal—

Kids forgive your daddy
Mom you don't have to marry
The heart will still beat
    With me
    And her
                           And him
                      with us as one
                  An orchestral unison,

Love is forever what keeps the step graced
Redundant my words, but correctly they're placed...

        Global instillment
       The goal, my fulfillment
  A role wrapped like this poem
     Entwined with my soul!

ABOUT THE AUTHOR

Ka-Son was born in Bed-Stuy and raised in the Flatbush section of Brooklyn, New York. Although he was raised by a single mother, his father played a big role in his life. He spent many weekends and summers at his father's apartment in Bed-Stuy. There, when he wasn't practicing his gymnastics with his brothers in vacant lots on old mattresses, he cultivated his natural artistic ability by watching the creative processes of his father, a portrait artist, and his eldest brother, a local Graffiti artist. Drawing and Graffiti writing became his passion.

Ka-Son believes he didn't get much literary instruction from the New York public school system. In fact, the school system had an adverse effect on his education, despite having an "A" average in elementary school. Thus, to the teachers he became invisible. A bout with the chicken pox in high school forced him to miss his English finals. To make up for it, he was kindly given an assignment by his English teacher. "She was a young, African American teacher who took a chance on me. I think she saw something in me that most in school didn't, that I was indeed bright, only very lazy". The assignment: one week to read and write a report on the book, "Wuthering Heights", or fail. "I guess I'm failing this class," he thought. To his surprise, the story drew him in, seeing a world and time totally different than his real life. That report was praised by the teacher, and a literary interest was sparked. The next year, a creative essay helped him gain the highest score in the school on the English Regents. "I was finally 'seen', although it came only right before graduation," he says.

So, he set out to prove that he wasn't a wasted mind. In college, he won second place in a short story contest, which was published in the local college anthology. He also wrote for the student newspaper. Along with his Graphic Design major's course load, he took extra courses in literature including Contemporary, African, English and Law through Literature. He graduated Magna Cum Laude from the City University of New York's Baccalaureate Program.

Education exposed him to works of different sorts by a myriad of authors. It was the concept of Love, however, and its ability to amplify just about all aspects of human emotion, that really charged creative inspiration. And from first-hand experience he wrote, and wrote, and wrote. And he hasn't stopped. For him, writing has become sort of a Self-discovery, a path for the mind to walk toward self-growth.

www.ingramcontent.com/pod-product-compliance
Lightning Source LLC
Chambersburg PA
CBHW022359040426
42450CB00005B/253